JOHN C
POWYS

To my Wife

JOHN COWPER POWYS

Herbert Williams

Border Lines Series Editor
John Powell Ward

seren

seren is the book imprint of
Poetry Wales Press Ltd
Wyndham Street, Bridgend
CF31 1EF Wales

A CIP record for this book is available at the
British Library CIP Office

ISBN 1-85411-196-5
1-85411-197-3 paperback

The publisher acknowledges the financial support of the Arts Council of Wales

Cover photograph reproduced
by permission of the Powys Society

Printed in Palatino by
Cromwell Press, Melksham, Wiltshire

Contents

List of Illustrations

Part One:
Life-Illusion

One

John Cowper Powys was an extraordinary man whose work arouses strong passions. Some critics see him as a literary genius, while others are dismissive of his achievements. Arguments over the value of his work are unlikely to abate quickly, but there is no disputing the prodigality of his output nor the range it encompasses. While predominantly a novelist, he was also a poet, literary critic and essayist. He ventured into drama, the vitality of his early work suggesting that he might have made a successful playwright had he been so inclined. As a diarist and letter writer, he had few equals either in terms of productivity or vigour of expression. In the art of the spoken word, too, he excelled: for many years he earned his living as a lecturer on the highly demanding American circuit, holding audiences spellbound and commanding high fees.

To see Powys solely in terms of literary or thespian performance, however, is to confine him to far too narrow a frame. He devised a personal philosophy which has had a profound effect on the lives of many, and possessed a charisma which impressed all who met him. There was, too, a suspicion of occult powers about him. From his childhood he saw himself as something of a magician, and although he only flirted with the black arts, there were occasions when he appears to have projected an image of himself over a distance by some unexplained psychic process.

Powys was English by birth but from an early age felt an affinity with Wales. This was undoubtedly inspired by his father's proud claim to be descended from the ancient princes of Powys, notably 'Rhodri Mawr, King of All Wales'. What some regarded as a harmless obsession took a surprising turn when, at the age of sixty-two, he settled in North Wales with his companion Phyllis Playter. They lived first at Corwen and then at Blaenau Ffestiniog, where he died in 1963 in his ninety-first year. It could be argued that this was proof not only of the strength of his belief in himself as a 'Welsh aboriginal' but of his claim to be something of a magician. A magician, he would argue, creates his own reality, and in shaping himself into a Welshman — or at least a 'Cymric' — as convincingly as he could, Powys showed a creative genius at least as strong as any he brought to his novels.

John Cowper Powys was born in the Derbyshire village of Shirley on 8 October 1872, the eldest of the eleven children of the Rev Charles Francis Powys and Mary Cowper Powys, née Johnson. Charles's pride in his supposed Welsh descent cannot obscure the fact that for centuries the Powyses had been country gentlemen living in Shropshire, proud enough of their status to put their family crest on their cutlery. By becoming a Church of England cleric Charles followed in the footsteps of his father, the Rev Littleton Charles Powys, who was rector of Stalbridge in Dorset. There were parsons on the distaff side, too, but the Johnsons were more obviously 'literary' in their tastes. Their pride was in sharing the blood not of princes but poets, for they claimed collateral descent from John Donne and William Cowper. Whether this has anything other than genealogical significance is hard to say. There are those who see in the Johnson inheritance the seeds of the remarkable flowering of literary talent among the offspring of Charles and Mary Powys, who included not only John Cowper Powys but Theodore Francis Powys and Llewelyn Powys, both of whom achieved literary fame. A Powys biographer Kenneth Hopkins, however, has been disdainful of this argument, noting that the blood relationship with Cowper comes through his second cousin, the Rev John Johnson, 'a man who was Cowper's exact opposite in temperament', and that the Donne connection 'is additionally weakened by its remoteness in time' (TPB, 2).

Such disputes cannot cloud the fact that the Rev Charles Francis Powys and his wife raised a family of gifted children who expressed themselves in varied ways. Philippa Powys, known as Katie, was a novelist and poet, A.R. Powys (Bertie) an architect and author of books relating to his profession, Marian (May) an authority on lace, Gertrude an artist and Littleton a sportsman and lifelong naturalist who for eighteen years was headmaster of Sherborne Preparatory School. All the boys in the family turned out to be writers of some kind or another with the exception of the youngest, William, who farmed in Kenya and became a spare-time painter. The other children were Lucy and Eleanor (Nellie). Lucy's love of literature proved an inspiration for her daughter Mary, who wrote poetry and fiction under her married name of Mary Casey, but Eleanor had no chance to fulfil herself, dying of appendicitis at the age of thirteen.

The family itself, and his position in it, are central to our understanding of John Cowper Powys. To the outsider it could assume a corporate identity that was daunting. Louis Marlow, the nom-de-plume of Powys's close friend Louis Wilkinson, found it a 'formidable phenomenon ... there seemed something preposterous and unallowable about this great strong thick wall of Powys solidarity, as though it stood there blasphemous against the solidarity of the human race' (WA, 3). The dominant force was the father, Charles Francis Powys, whose powerful personality imposed itself on the household like the strictures of a minor deity. Marlow, indeed, likened him to 'some dim prehistoric god' creating a sense of family in which the children could both merge and flower individually. In contrast, the mother was a sensitive and even morbid woman, affectionate in a reserved way but (in Marlow's opinion) hateful of success and shying from displays of high spirits. She too could impose her will on her children, less energetically than her husband but no less implacably. It is revealing of much in her personality that she is said to have preferred to walk in the shade than in the sun, and to carry a white foxglove rather than a coloured one.

To be the first-born in such a family must have been no easy task, but in spite of his complex personality John Cowper Powys appeared untroubled by the role. He took the liberty of teasing not only Littleton, two years his junior, but his younger brothers and sisters. The unquestioned leadership he showed at the age of nine in dragooning his siblings into the 'Volentia Army' of which he was commander-in-chief expressed itself less dictatorially in adult life, but he remained the chief among equals. Perhaps the status of first-born of such a man as C.F. Powys gave him an inner security that served him well in his struggles with the dark forces within him which he details so honestly in his writings.

Although only the first seven years of his life were spent in Shirley, he remained conscious of his native county to the end of his days. A former neighbour in Blaenau Ffestiniog recalls how Powys, by then an octogenarian, would say delightedly, 'I have the Derbyshire spring in me!' In fact, Powys devoted the first chapter of his *Autobiography* to his infancy in the gently undulating countryside south of Dovedale, now part of the Peak District National Park. He describes

Dovedale itself in glowing and even fanciful terms, conjuring up a picture of 'steep and very often cavernous precipices' mounting up on both sides of 'a stream that might be compared to a falcon in dove's feathers'. Familiar with Greek legend from his schooldays in Sherborne, he came to liken that part of Derbyshire centring around the Peak to the boss of a Homeric shield, the villages near the town of Ashbourne forming the shield's margin.

Shirley is one of those villages. It stands on a slight incline amid a network of country lanes just off the busy A52 that runs from Ashbourne to Derby. St Michael's Church, where the Rev C.F. Powys was vicar from 1872-79, is to be found almost opposite the Saracen's Head, a sturdy pub dating from 1791. A panel inside the fourteenth century church listing all the rectors and vicars shows Powys senior to have been the thirty-second incumbent, succeeding Eardley Wilmot Michell, who was vicar for twenty-five years. The vicarage where John Cowper Powys was born, now known as the Old Vicarage and privately owned, is a few hundred yards east of the village proper and reached by a lane that joins the A52 a short distance from the house. Powys remembered it as 'a square whitish-yellow building' but it is rectangular rather than square, a handsome low-roofed dwelling reputedly built in 1824. He claimed to have no recollection at all of the church but vividly recalled the day when, walking the high-hedged lane leading down to it, he astonished the nursemaid pushing Littleton's pram by declaring himself to be 'the Lord of Hosts'. Most of his early memories, however, centred on the vicarage and its surrounding shrubberies, in which his father energetically laboured as a relief from his studies and parish duties. This 'tall, powerful man in black clothes' trimmed laurel bushes, the 'enormously thick' soles of his boots making a great impression on the boy. Nearly sixty years later John Cowper Powys, again playing the magician who transmutes the mundane into the extraordinary, was conscious of 'some wonderful secret of happiness' while contemplating his father's boot-soles, although the secret eluded him whenever he tried to grasp it.

It would be hard to exaggerate the importance of the Rev C.F. Powys in the life of his eldest son. He was a Colossus bestriding the world of shrubberies and spinneys on which the imagination of Johnny Powys first began to feed. One has the impression of a stern but not over-severe man who disdained the sadistic punishments which darkened so many childhoods in Victorian times. There were none of the savage beatings which 'God-fearing' fathers justified by pointing to the Old Testament instruction never to spare the rod. The worst physical punishment he meted out was a violent box on the ear, and after leaving Shirley even this habit fell into disuse. Occasionally he resorted to more unusual punishments which he felt best fitted the crime. After hearing his first-born son's cot shake night after night with what John Cowper Powys recalls as 'the feverish intensity of my infantile eroticism,' he would ask the boy next morning: 'Have you been doing that?' In spite of the touching honesty of the admission that he had indeed been 'doing that', young Johnny did not escape being douched with ice-cold water. There was, perhaps, a ferocity in C.F. Powys's nature kept severely under control. Louis Marlow remarks on the 'wolf-like implications of his face and the grim resistant Parta Tueri line of his mouth' (WA, 4). He took intense pleasure simply in being alive, contemplating the drama of his own existence. To his children he communicated his passionate love of the natural world, teaching them the names of flowers and plants and giving them a sense of the sheer wonder of being alive on this planet. A man of his time in the simplicity of his religious faith, he was equally so in his enthusiasms. He took pride in his collection of birds' eggs but instructed his sons always to leave two eggs in the nest, and to put a hooked fish out of its misery rather than let it lie 'flapping and gasping on the bank'.

Perhaps the greatest favour C.F. Powys did his eldest son was to instil in him a love of storytelling. Every day, following afternoon tea at Shirley, he would sit on the drawing-room sofa with his sons John, Littleton and Theodore and tell them an endless tale about two mythical personalities, Giant Grumble and Fairy Sprightly. The villain of the piece was, significantly, a pedantic scientist called The Professor, 'whose sinister activities required all the arts of both Giant and Fairy to circumvent and neutralize' (*Autobiography*, 4). In this never-ending story we can see the seeds of the long romances, dealing often in the conflict between good and evil, in the writing of which John Cowper Powys displayed his particular genius.

C.F. Powys was undoubtedly an affectionate and considerate parent but there was a strange intensity in him which made him at times an awesome and even menacing figure. In the probably autobiographical early chapters of Llewelyn Powys's novel *Apples Be Ripe*, the Rev Thomas Holbech (the C.F. Powys figure) is pictured as a proud and reserved man whose 'whole being could tremble with a purely animal gusto for life'. His son Chris (Llewelyn), hiding behind a syringa bush, sees his father's

> noble countenance contorted by a mad and uncontrollable animal transport, for no better reason than that he was alive in such fair weather ... Chris had been terrified. He had looked at that unknown face, elongated, baboon-like, and before the violence of so abnormal an emotion he could only hold his breath in awe.
>
> (ABR, 9-11)

There was, perhaps, more holding of breath at Shirley, and later at Montacute, than has been admitted.

From his earliest days, John Cowper Powys was apt to give objects and elements of the natural scene a symbolic meaning. An axe fashioned by his father out of laurel wood and given him on an emotionally charged occasion emanated 'a glamour of fairy-tale enchantment'.

> To get back that laurel-axe from that garden spinney at Shirley would now be to get back the full magical power of that timeless fetish-worship of which the quaintest, most ordinary object — a tree-stump, a pile of stones, a pool by the roadside, an ancient chimney-stack — can become an Ark of the Covenant, evocative of the Music of the Spheres!
>
> (*Autobiography*, 3)

This, hyperbolic though it may seem, is quintessential Powys, the rapturous evocation of a mood which in its intensity recalls the 'animal transport' displayed in the face of the Rev Thomas Holbech. There was symbolism, too, in the oddly-shaped hill on the southern fringe of Dovedale which he knew as Mount Cloud (correctly, Thorpe Cloud). This conical hill 287 metres high, its grassy slopes stippled with pale limestone rock, induced a 'dim feeling of *immensity*' in his young mind and fifty years later remained 'synonymous with sublimity'. It excited the boy so much that he scrabbled at the damp soil alongside the vicarage drive with his bare hands, modelling one 'Mount Cloud' after another and covering them with moss. The son is father to the man; for in his old age Powys would be equally stirred by the mountain he could see from the window of his quarryman's cottage in Blaenau Ffestiniog, which he fancifully — and typically — likened to Mount Olympus.

Ecstasies over Mount Cloud notwithstanding, Johnny Powys (who was later to become Jack and later still plain John) was not a happy child; or at least, he did not recall being such. Most of the incidents he remembered from his infancy in Shirley were of 'shameful, destructive and grotesque' events, although his penchant for self-dramatisation enabled him to make much of very little. He was once discovered blithely scooping up tadpoles from a deep pond and putting them into shallow puddles, and there was the rudimentary masturbation implicit in the cot-shaking; all such misdemeanours incurred the wrath of his father. More seriously, he half-strangled his brother Littleton while playing hangman with a bell-rope. He claimed to have no recollection of the punishment meted out to him then but parental disapproval, however justified, must have played some part in shaping the secret terrors he endured. 'My whole life ... has been one long struggle with Fear, self-created fantastical Fear,' he confessed (*Autobiography*, 12). It expressed itself agonisingly after a picnic at Osmaston Park, when he threw a stick in the lake and was told he had better look out, or the police would have him! The thoughtless words, tossed away as casually as the stick upon the water, caused the sensitive boy endless suffering, for night after night he lay awake fearing the police would come for him and take him away.

What caused Powys most misery in childhood, however, and for a large part of his adult life, was the fatal allure of sadistic images. One of his admissions in his confession-laden *Autobiography* is that he could not recall a time when 'sadistic thoughts and images did not disturb and intoxicate me'. He recalls the guilty pleasure he took in gazing at a picture of an eagle seizing a lamb which he found in one of his nursery storybooks; such lurid illustrations in works expressly designed for young children were commonplace not only in Victorian times but well into the twentieth century. Sadism, 'the most dangerous of all vices', plagued him until the age of fifty, when he overcame it by never allowing himself to derive any pleasure from it. It must be emphasised that this was a sadism almost wholly of the imagination, for the only cruelties he deliberately perpetrated were against small creatures in his childhood. To the crime of transferring tadpoles from deep to shallow pools can be added the further offence of torturing worms: the kind of behaviour in which many small boys indulge without being overwhelmed by remorse. For one of Powys's sensibilities, however, the perverted pleasure obtained from the mere visualising of brutalities was itself a great wickedness. The belief in the efficacy of psychic forces which runs like an undercurrent through his mature work led him to believe that intense mental concentration of this kind creates magnetic vibrations which leave an 'evil impress' on the surrounding air. 'Thoughts, as Paracalsus taught, when they are visualized and brooded on for a long while, *tend to become entities*.' The eidola of such imaginations, he suggested, might affect other minds. Powys variously described this forbidden pleasure as a quiver of the evil nerve, sweet poison, a deadly shiver, an ambiguous thrill, a sinister flame, even 'sweet, abominable Dead-Sea fruit'. One cannot help remarking that in roundly condemning the vice, he succeeds in making it sound damnably attractive.

Powys's self-torture is reflected most powerfully in his fiction through the character of Owen Evans, the tall, gaunt Welshman in *A Glastonbury Romance* whose 'poisoned and brackish' senses are redeemed only when he marries. Evans owns an antiquarian bookshop but forces himself not to read one particular volume which he keeps locked away. He is troubled by the recurring image of a killing blow delivered by an iron bar. The scenes of sadistic cruelty dwelling in the back chambers of his mind have an extraordinary effect on him, making 'his pulses beat, his blood dance, his senses swoon, his knees knock together'.

> The taste of the least of these loathsome scenes was so overpowering to him that it reduced all the rest of life — eating, drinking, working, playing, walking, talking — to tedious occurrences, that had to be got through but that were wanting entirely in the electric quiver of real excitement. What Mr Evans suffered from was a fever of remorse such as cannot very often have taken possession of human minds in the long course of history. To say that the unhappy man wished that he had never been born would be to put his case mildly. Like Othello he longed to bathe in 'steep-down gulfs of liquid fire'.
> (AGR, 109)

The extent to which Powys projected his own sufferings on to those of Evans can only be imagined. There is no doubt, however, that the sweet poison of sadism ran strongly enough in his veins to make him fearful of the effects of fictional cruelty on impressionable minds. The 'loathsome scenes' that so excited Evans are only hinted at, for Powys was a man with the most troublesome of consciences. Self-absorbed, forever grappling with the mystery of identity, he was easily driven to self-disgust. Wilfully to cause hurt, not only to human beings but to any living creature, was for him an abomination. He was appalled by vivisection and scornful of the arguments used to justify it. His sympathy extended also to what is commonly regarded as the insensate world of plants; in his novels he accords sensations, even memories, to trees. Stones, earth, even man-created objects like walls; for him they were all presences, with identities to be honoured. And he seems, in a sense, to encompass all things to his admirers. It is not that he was a god; nor even god-like; but that his comprehensive sympathy and dignity make him a symbol of the essential worth of all things under the sun.

Two

> The Sea lost nothing of the swallowing identity of its great outer mass of waters in the emphatic, individual character of each particular wave. Each wave, as it rolled in upon the high-pebbled beach, was an epitome of the whole body of the sea, and carried with it all the vast mysterious quality of the earth's ancient antagonist.
>
> (WS, 17)

These opening sentences of John Cowper Powys's *Weymouth Sands* reveal not only his taste for a grand beginning to those huge, sprawling novels which he liked to think of as 'romances' but also his feelings for the sea; in particular the sea that laps the shores of Weymouth and its environs. He wrote the book in his early sixties but its roots lie in his experience of the town in his early childhood, when he was taken on visits to his paternal grandmother.

Amelia Powys (born Amelia Moilliet) lived in Penn House, a bow-windowed terraced house in The Esplanade on Weymouth's sea front. In time it became the Penn House Hotel and a place of pilgrimage for Powysians, as admirers of the Powys family in all its tribal glory rather cosily describe themselves. It was here that John Cowper Powys experienced sensations which would not only colour his novels but play an important part in the philosophy of life he was to evolve. They were related partly to his senses and partly to the inner world into which he was learning to withdraw. He was especially enamoured of a room full of early Victorian bric-à-brac, a room with a peculiar smell that mingled with the 'smells of seaweed and fish and sun-warmed pebbles that came in through those large bow windows'. He was intoxicated also by the smell of the passage wafted to him when, after an outing with his parents, the door of Penn House was opened.

> To my childish senses there was a constant interpenetration

> between the whole seashore and the interior of this house; the spray and the foam and the jelly-fish and the starfish floating in and floating out all the while, and carrying my consciousness backwards and forwards with them between objects of art from India and the enchanted sands beyond the donkey-stand.
> (*Autobiography*, 20)

The objects of art from India were brought to Weymouth by his Uncle Littleton, his father's elder brother, a captain in the 59th Regiment who impressed young Johnny Powys with his courage by allowing the child to pound his bearded face with his fists during visits to Shirley. This officer of the Queen died of cholera in Afghanistan in 1879, a tragedy which precipitated Charles Francis Powys's decision to move his family from Shirley to Dorchester in order that he might be near his widowed mother. By then the Powyses already had five children under eight, seven-year-old John Cowper being the elder brother of Littleton Charles, five; Theodore Francis, four; Gertrude, two, and Eleanor (Nelly), a baby of a few months.

Charles's move to his native Dorset could not have been made without much heart-searching, as it meant a decline in his status. Instead of being Vicar of St Michael's in Shirley, a position made all the more authoritative because the village lacked a squire, he became a mere curate to the Rector of St Peter's in Dorchester, the chief church in this urban parish. His eldest son, although far too young to appreciate social nuances at the time, was in due course to refer to this temporary demotion as 'a rather unworldly move in a young priest's life'. Any blow to the pride of Charles Francis Powys, however, would have been cushioned not only by the satisfaction of displaying filial duty to his mother but by the acquisition of the £40,000 family fortune which came to him on the death of his brother. This enabled him to take on the lease of Rothesay House, a grand new 'brick and mortar castle' near the South Walk built especially to his requirements. So grand was it, in fact, that the local rector used to point it out to his friends as an edifice far beyond the expectations of most curates.

John Cowper Powys was wont to describe himself as a 'sensationalist', a thrilling awareness of his own existence as a sensate being forming a vital part of his personality from childhood. He experienced ecstasies as a child, sometimes inspired by the sight of the sun glittering on the sea as he gazed through the bow windows of Penn House. He also learned the trick of conjuring up a myriad colours by pressing his knuckles into his eyes. More satisfying still was the sensation of sinking down deeply into himself, a practice which in time he was to ascribe to his fictional character Wolf Solent. It gave him the sense of engaging in an 'occult mental struggle' between good and evil in the remote depths of his being, and he called it his 'mythology'.

In exchanging the narrow village life of Shirley for the urban environments of first Weymouth and then Dorchester, Charles Francis Powys enabled his son to gain access to a wider world. There were encounters with the elderly poet William Barnes, who regularly strolled beneath the chestnut trees of Dorchester's South Walk 'dressed, in the style of a hundred years ago, in knee-breeches, black stockings, and silver-buckled shoes'. Thomas Hardy lived half a mile away in Max Gate, although some years were to elapse before John Cowper Powys came to know him socially. The most vivid impressions of Dorchester arose, however, not from human encounters but from the stories his father told him of its history. Looking from his bedroom window in Rothesay House one midsummer evening, the boy was startled to see what he took to be a procession of phantoms moving mechanically along South Walk. They were, in reality, simply ordinary passers-by, which his imagination had transformed into the likeness of ghosts of the French prisoners who had planted the chestnut trees along the town's Walks at the time of the Napoleonic Wars. Although most children are prone to feverish imaginings at one time or another, such experiences had lasting significance for Powys, who claimed to have 'always been one to expect, and to accept, marvels and wonders, as part of what might be called the natural "chaoticism" of the world.'

Although, by his own confession, a 'nervous, strung-up' child, this did not prevent him exerting authority over his younger brothers and sisters. It was at Rothesay House, in his ninth year, that he dragooned them into joining his imaginary Volentia Army. Typically, he came to insist that this was no mere childish pursuit but something surrounded by the mythological: 'a sort of secret Rosicrucian, or Thaumaturgic society, of which I — a young Prester John — was the head.' By this time he was attending a dame's school in Dorchester, and the fact that he was able to enlist all his fellow-pupils into his army as well as his siblings speaks much for the force of his personality.

Such happiness as he was able to derive from pursuits of this kind was snatched from him by his father's decision to send him away to boarding school, the customary cruelty which the English upper middle classes inflict on their sons and, sometimes, their daughters. The fatal year was 1883, when John was a little short of his eleventh birthday and his brother Littleton, who was to share this experience, nine. The chosen school was Westbury House, a preparatory school in the small town of Sherborne from which boys generally proceeded to Sherborne School itself. The day of his departure from Rothesay House was branded indelibly on John Cowper Powys's mind, for it meant that he and his brother were plunging 'into stresses and tensions, shocks and endurances, the like of which, unless they went to war or became penniless outcasts, they would never again have to experience till the day of their death.' Opposite them in the railway carriage sat their broad-shouldered father, who kept any emotions he might have been feeling to himself.

> How well I remember waking up in the grey dawn on our first morning in the Prep., and staring at Littleton's calm sleep in wonder, till at last, under my stare, his eyes opened too, and then, oh! what great, round, *slow* tears I saw rolling down his manful cheeks! Littleton's bed and mine were side by side; while W—'s bed was just opposite mine, on the other side of the room. W— did, I confess, display in one respect what most authorities would have regarded as praiseworthy 'reliability'; for when in the hushed hours of the night there came the smallest movement from my bed that could be interpreted as 'sinful' he would send one of his heavy slippers flying at my head.
>
> (*Autobiography*, 80)

Looking back half a century, Powys saw the person he identified only as 'W—' as a quiet, reliable boy who for all his virtues derived some sensual satisfaction from the exercise of authority in certain unspecified ways. In the spirit of scrupulous honesty which he brought to the writing of his *Autobiography*, Powys confessed to sharing this vice and suggested that practically every 'dispenser of punishment' (by implication, corporal punishment) also enjoyed 'sensual stirrings' while meting it out.

Lacking all interest in football and cricket at a time when the concept of muscular Christianity had infiltrated all institutions attended by the offspring of the well-to-do, Powys was singularly unsuited to life in prep school. Yet, thanks to being put in charge of the small school library by the headmaster, W.H. Blake, he maintains that he was 'often extremely happy at the Preparatory'. Although initially a slow learner who could not read until he was seven and a half, he was now able to indulge his love of books and soak himself in such authors as Jules Verne, thrilling to the adventures of Captain Nemo. These moments of happiness, however, stemmed not from his acceptance of Prep School ethos but from his defiance of it. Significantly, he tells us that his dominant desire during the whole of his schooldays was to lead a double life, just about getting by in the school dimension but finding his real happiness in a secret world where he was monarch of all he surveyed. For all his talk of occasional happiness, one cannot avoid the feeling that John Cowper Powys's schooldays were on the whole an experience made endurable only by the exercise of an already powerful imagination.

> As I say, my chief preoccupation at school — whether in the Prep. or the Big School — was to live as if I were *at home and not at school*; and in this, considering the difficulties I encountered, I was really wonderfully successful.
> (*Autobiography*, 87)

It was, no doubt, good training for a novelist, and a fertile breeding ground for the philosophy which Powys evolved of the duality of good and evil in the First Cause. Much comfort was also derived from the companionship of his brother Littleton, a natural athlete who was later to become headmaster of Sherborne Prep. The two boys took long Sunday afternoon walks through country lanes, walks which tended to veer in the direction of the home which John missed so abominably. They were especially fond of the area known as The Trent Lanes, a network of narrow grassy lanes between the main road to Yeovil and the village of Trent. John also had a rather morbid interest in a supposedly bottomless pond which may have been the inspiration for the Lenty Pond of ill repute in his novel *Wolf Solent*.

The bullying endemic in school life of any kind troubled him increasingly as he approached his twelfth birthday. It turned him into something of a bully himself although, one suspects, not a very successful one. The latent sadism in him was encouraged by the canings which were commonplace at Sherborne Prep. John and Littleton were caned only once by headmaster Blake (absurdly, for depicting caning in a painting or drawing produced in one of their art lessons) but others were not so fortunate. It is difficult to accept John Cowper Powys's assertion that Blake was untouched by the vice of sadism when one hears how he inflicted black and blue stripes on small boys, who proudly displayed them to their fellow-pupils before lights out in their dorm. It was at Prep School that he decided to grow up to be a poet, a vow that shook him with a 'transporting ecstasy,' yet the dull weight of the oppression that for the most part bore down on him is summarised by his reflection that

> ... is it not a strange thing, how, if you are an Englishman of the upper-middle class, you suffer the greatest hardships of your life before you are twelve years old? School in England — the Public School system — has a hundred times a greater influence over you than Oxford or Cambridge or any other University. My own brothers differ greatly between themselves over this question of the Public School system, Littleton, who greatly enjoyed it, upholding it steadily, and Llewelyn, who also enjoyed it, attacking it fiercely. My own attitude is, I fancy, not very different from the attitude of many ex-soldiers. I would not like to condemn others to such experiences; but I am proud, in a sense, to have gone through them myself!
> (*Autobiography*, 92)

In 1885 John and Littleton progressed to the 'Big School' of Sherborne, an ancient institution which was originally a monastic school founded by St Aeldhelm in the year AD 705. They were placed in the house presided over by William Beauchamp Wildman, a philologist and antiquary whom John came to see as a rare eccentric. He had little idea of how to control turbulent boys on the brink of adolescence, sometimes showing extreme tolerance and on other occasions falling on them in a fury. It was in Wildman's that John Cowper Powys encountered the worst bully he had ever known, someone he hated so much that at the age of sixty he declared himself willing to 'plunge into a physical contest with him'. There were, however, moments of happiness when on Sunday afternoons he sat in the school library, luxuriating in its tranquillity as he contentedly searched this treasure house of books ancient and modern. On the surface he was a successful pupil, for whom examinations posed no terror, but one generally has the sense of misery being piled on misery for a boy who stood out so clearly as an oddity that he was known as 'Moony'. His days at Sherborne ended abruptly and in an extraordinary fashion. One Sunday afternoon, when Wildman was away, a crowd of pupils whom Powys categorised as 'a mob' threw open the door of the study he shared with Littleton and began pushing one another in. His inability to strike an honest blow to dispel them, and the way his fear infected Littleton, became a lifelong cause for shame. Yet there was pride in what followed, for during the evening service in chapel he resolved to fight back in his own way. His counter-attack took the form of a tumultuous speech, delivered impromptu after the boys' supper of beer and bread and cheese, in which he mocked himself in inspired fashion.

> I dragged in every single detail they derided me for, I exposed my lacerations, my shames, my idiocies. 'Moony' was talking at last out of the madness of the mistress of his horoscope! I referred to the great dilapidated umbrella I placed such stock in. I referred to my obscene fashion of chewing my food with my front teeth. I stripped myself naked before them. Taliessin himself could not have prophesied to such a tune when he celebrated the procession of his planetary metamorphoses.
> (*Autobiography*, 155)

When he sat down there was a moment's silence, followed by wild applause. Moony, the outcast, who had once performed a 'manic dance' to save himself from a bully, had at last triumphed. But the physical and mental effort involved in this classic turning of the tables took its toll, and next day Powys Major lay wanly in the sick-room at Sherborne, plagued by the gastric trouble that was to prove a lifelong torment. The carriage came to take him home and he made only one appearance as a pupil at Sherborne thereafter. That too was a triumph, as on the last day of term he recited his prize English poem on the subject of Corinth:

> Superbly huge, majestically steep,
> The Citadel looks down with steadfast eye;
> About its base the careless seagulls fly,
> Seeking their rocky homes secure from harm;
> While over sea and land there reigns a deathless calm.

Three

By this time the Powys family had moved again: to Montacute, a village of striking beauty in south-east Somerset, only a short distance from Yeovil. The move from Dorchester came about through the patronage of the village squire, William R. Phelips, who appointed Charles Francis Powys vicar of St Catherine's Church in 1885. It was a change much to the liking of Powys Major of Sherborne School, who as the gate of the drive swung to behind him one evening, gravely told his father how much he admired the leafy approach to their new house. Rubbing his hands together in delight at this unexpected praise, Charles replied with equal portentousness: 'I'm very glad, John, my boy, that you appreciate the home I have provided for you!'

The beauty of Montacute derives from its being built of the honey-coloured stone quarried at Ham Hill, just outside the village. This hill, gouged and split by centuries of quarrying, appears as Leo's Hill in John Cowper Powys's early novel *Wood and Stone* and the village itself is fictionalised as Nevilton, after the Nevils who were the seigneurs of Montacute in ancient times. Llewelyn Powys, a much warmer and more sensual writer than his elder brother, was moved to ecstasy by the sight of Ham Hill stone and its historical associations with labouring men of successive generations, but John Cowper Powys showed his appreciation in much cooler fashion:

> The sandstone of Leo's Hill remains, so architects tell us, the only rival of granite, as a means for the perpetuation of human monuments. Even granite wears less well than this, in respect to the assaults of rain and flood .... As far as Nevilton itself is concerned everything in the place owes its persuasive texture to this resistant yet soft material. From the lordly Elizabethan mansion to the humblest pig-stye, they all proceed from the entrails of Leo's Hill; and they all wear — these motley whelps

> of the great dumb beast — its tawny skin, its malleable sturdiness, its enduring consistence.
> (WAS, 4)

The Powyses settled naturally into their ordained place in the society of Montacute, joining the magic circle around the comfortable figure of William Phelips. A distance was thus fixed between themselves and the more humble villagers, however assiduously the new vicar might perform his parish duties. There were hints of an older aristocracy, however, in the presence of 'tall, stately labouring men, with the gaunt frames and hooked noses of the Bayeux Tapestry.' These were descendants of the once-proud Nevils, by then as extinct as Thomas Hardy's fictional d'Urbevilles. Coming to Montacute from the Roman remains of Dorchester was, for John Cowper Powys, 'like plunging into the earth-mould of medieval romance'. He revelled in the splendour of Montacute House, although the more critical Llewelyn remembered the presence still in the fields of clearly legible notices saying 'Beware of Man Traps'. His brother John preferred to recall the more jovial side of the squire, who bluffly exclaimed 'We are being chaffed by the populace!' as the village boys raised a shout at the sight of the Phelips carriage lumbering through the spacious square, quaintly known as The Borough. John Cowper Powys saw Phelips as a learned and somewhat eccentric gentleman whose peculiarity of manners and speech made a great impression on him. 'He was,' notes Powys disarmingly, 'the first person I ever heard utter the words 'By Jove!'

It is in the setting of Montacute that the Powys family first come alive for us; more particularly, in the vicarage. We see them sitting at table, the paterfamilias gravely saying prayers before a morsel of breakfast could be eaten. For Louis Marlow it was a daunting sight, the Powys family being an entity of peculiar power. He saw the table itself as warranting an initial capital in his recollections of being seated there, marooned in a sea of Powyses.

> That Table was a formidable phenomenon. Sitting at it, I felt perturbingly single-handed, an alien invader without the ghost of a chance. I felt that I belonged to an entirely different race. If I could have changed my pigmentation and the colour of my hair to something more Powys-like, I should have felt safer.
>
> I was not only nonplussed but resentful; for there seemed

> something preposterous and unallowable about this great strong thick wall of Powys solidarity, as though it stood there blasphemous against the solidarity of the human race. As 'anti-social' as the family motto Parta Tueri.
> (WA, 3)

For Isobel Powys Marks, who first visited Montacute Vicarage as a child in 1908, the head of this overwhelming tribe was a remote figure fond of country walks who invariably brought something back from the hedgerows, be it a flower or a twig or a shell. In her eighties she also retained clear memories of the house itself, especially the way the ground-floor sash windows came down almost to floor level so that if the lower half were raised 'one could go into the sitting room and the dining room directly from the garden'. The daughter of the sixth Powys child, the architect Albert Reginald Powys, she recalled how the Rev Charles Francis Powys invariably referred to the three female servants at this time as 'the maidens,' and how they would seat themselves near the table for family prayers, after which the food would be brought in and the head of the household would himself ladle out the porridge.

The ties of home were strong enough to persuade John Cowper and Littleton to go to extreme lengths to snatch an hour or two there at weekends while at Sherborne. They discovered that it was possible to run to Montacute and back on certain Sunday afternoons in the summer term, 'between our regular school dinner which was over before two, and our regular school tea which did not begin till six'. Since it was ten miles each way, the excursion demanded no small degree of athleticism as well as enthusiasm. Once safely in the vicarage, they tucked into strawberries 'squashed up, after our bucolic fashion, with milk and sugar' and were in time for bread and butter tea in Wildman's House on their return.

John Cowper's schoolboy days ended in the summer of 1891, when his father arrived in a hired carriage to take him home after his outburst over supper. A few months later they made the journey together to Cambridge, where John Cowper followed his father and both grandfathers in becoming a student at Corpus Christi. In later life he claimed to remember nothing of their initial interviews with the authorities, although he clearly categorised the Cambridge dons as middle-aged men wholly immersed in their well-established lives. The lively imagination which had persuaded him to see

Montacute as something out of medieval romance now influenced his thinking on Corpus. The Old Court, which his rooms overlooked, was like 'some enchanted ruin in a fairy-like forest of old romance'. It thrilled him to think that the Elizabethan dramatist Christopher Marlowe had once had his rooms there, and in this relic of medieval scholasticism he saw himself as 'swimming about in a bottomless pond of antiquity'. He relished the very act of dining in hall like his predecessors, glancing up now and then at the portraits on the panelled walls. All this speaks of a deep conservatism in John Cowper Powys, curiously at odds with the sympathy with communism which he was to profess later in life. Grotesquely, he found himself lumped with the 'rowing set' at Corpus on the strength of his father's prowess on the river Cam, although as it was a choice only between this and two other categories, the 'fast set' and the 'pietistic evangelical set', such labelling was not to be taken seriously.

The oddity that had marked him out at Sherborne was equally in evidence at Cambridge. He invited all comers to his rooms to hear a prophetic denunciation which he called Corpus Unveiled. Even the athletes turned up, eager for sensation. He also surprised a rather dull fellow-student with whom he was taking a walk by launching into an inspired defence of the Trinity, all the more disconcerting in one who professed no interest whatever in God or Christ. This was nothing, however, beside the trick he pulled in his first days at Corpus, when a bunch of unruly third year students who had set out to rag him found themselves looking down the barrel of a loaded revolver. He had conspired with his younger brother Theodore to buy the gun before going up to Cambridge, to ensure that he would not again suffer the kind of bullying he had endured at Sherborne. The weapon had been obtained, apparently without difficulty, at an ironmonger's in Yeovil, and was brought into service when word got around that freshmen at Corpus had their rooms invaded and their possessions thrown out of the window by the fast set. 'It was only necessary,' writes Powys laconically, 'to cause the mouth of this formidable weapon ... to emerge a brief distance from its hiding-place.'

In that leisurely age, when admission to our ancient universities depended on parental affluence rather than intellect, little pressure was put on undergraduates to exert themselves academically. The dons, reserved men pursuing quiet lives, maintained a spirit of sublime detachment in their dealings with students, allowing them to go to the devil in their own way, if they felt so inclined. Typically, John Cowper Powys, who was reading for the Historical Tripos, responded to this freedom not with orgies of self-indulgence but with the pursuit of asceticism. He became even more abstemious in his diet than his father, for whom stewed pears and rice pudding were the ultimate gourmet delights, and confessed in his *Autobiography* that when the porridge he cooked on the fire in his rooms tasted especially delicious, he would 'deliberately leave it in the pot for the delectation of the servant who cleaned my room'. Whether the servant availed himself of the opportunity of consuming it is anyone's guess, though Powys admitted that it might well have ended up as the cat's dinner. He also won parental approval by living even more frugally than his father had thought possible, 'one of the shortest cuts to his good graces'. But the most curious aspect of John Cowper's asceticism was his habit of seeking out the most unprepossessing of undergraduates to accompany him on his walks into the Cambridgeshire countryside. These took him to every point of the compass along straight, flat, monotonous roads, giving him the chance to engage in the long, long thoughts with which youth is traditionally imbued.

> What I am revealing to you now is the deepest and most essential secret of my life. My thoughts were lost in my sensations; and my sensations were of a kind so difficult to describe that I could write a volume upon them and still not really have put them down. But the field-dung upon my boots, the ditch-mud plastered thick, with little bits of dead grass in it, against the turned-up ends of my trousers, the feel of my oak-stick Sacred whose every indentation and corrugation and curve and knot and grain I knew as well as those on my hand, the salty taste of half-dried sweat upon my lips, the delicious swollenness of my fingers, the sullen sweet weariness of legs, the indescribably happiness of my calm, dazed, lulled, wind-drugged, air-drunk spirit, were all, after their kind, a sort of thinking, though of *exactly what*, it would be very hard for me to explain. Did I share at such times the sub-thoughts, or over-thoughts, that the old earth herself has, as she turns upon her axis, or that the vast volume of the ocean has, as his tide gathers along his beaches or draws back hoarsely into his gulfs?
> (*Autobiography*, 169)

This sense of being party to a secret which he found difficult to explain adequately was, he felt, the only real discovery he made while at Corpus. There were, however, blessings of a different kind, not least the absence of the sadistic thoughts which had plagued him since childhood. He was also free of his more normal 'mania' for pictures of sylph-like women with long legs. He came to see his Cambridge period as one of pure idealism, 'by far the most idyllic period of my life'. He had nothing to do with what he called 'society ladies' and few dealings with women of any kind. His ignorance was such that when he first learned of menstruation at Cambridge it came as a 'frightful shock'; even forty years later, when writing his Autobiography, he was driven to circumlocution, referring to 'the haemorrhages that women have to suffer from in the revolutions of the moon'. There was, however, an attempt at seduction, when he cajoled a young woman into bed (not, he emphasises, a bed within the monastic precincts of Corpus), but she failed a vital test in not possessing a sylph-like figure and he remained a virgin while she went away disappointed. The terra-cotta statues of nude divinities which he bought from a surprised Italian tradesmen were at once safer and more exciting than the imperfect limbs of real women; they satisfied, at one and the same time, his feverish desire to gaze at young women's limbs and his passion for classic mythology.

Years later, Llewelyn Powys came across the words 'Pray for the Soul of John Cowper Powys' emblazoned on a beam running across the ceiling of his brother's old chamber, but the impulse that suggested these words must have been a passing one. The truth is that while at Corpus, John Cowper Powys turned away from the Christian religion rather than towards it. He went up to Cambridge with the idea of becoming a clergyman, but changed his mind while he was there. His father accepted his decision without protest and, possibly, without surprise; he must already have had sufficient experience of the eclectic nature of his son's beliefs.

In the summer of 1894, John Cowper Powys went down from Cambridge with what he described as 'a very moderate Second Class' degree. He had made few close friends, admired only one of his university teachers, and had no idea what he wanted to do for a living. He had gained more knowledge of a bookish kind, enjoyed a welcome freedom from sadistic impulses and temporarily lost his fear of facing people. Most of all, he had developed the formidable mental power of being able to hide his real identity. Only when alone did he reveal his secret self, pouring forth his soul 'into such inanimate or such lowly-animate things as I could encounter along the most desolate country road.' Old posts, old heaps of stones, old haystacks thatched with straw, palings and hedges: these were his confidantes. For those more thoroughly immersed in student life he must have seemed as eccentric and lonely an individual as he had at Sherborne; but in the figure of this callow young man, striding the flat, long Cambridgeshire roads, we see the father of the novelist who has puzzled, vexed and inspired so many readers and critics since.

Four

There was no pressing need for John Cowper Powys to do anything after leaving Cambridge as his father, following the example of his own father before him, made him an allowance of £60 a year. Such a sum, at that time, would have enabled him to live temporarily in France, 'learning that language which I had been led to despise at Sherborne,' but for a son of C.F. Powys to live a life of idleness was unthinkable. Now that he had turned his back on the Church as a career his options were limited, but the well-established firm of Gabbitas and Thring came to his rescue. It sounded like a clutch of Dickensian lawyers, but was in fact an educational agency in London specialising in helping prep school headmasters to find assistants. Powys had no intention of becoming an assistant master (indeed, one wonders what he expected them to do for him), but by some freak of chance a German professor who lectured at girls' schools in Brighton had just died, thus leaving the way clear for the young graduate to step into his shoes. Whatever doubts Messrs Gabbitas and Thring may have had about offering the post to so callow a successor, Powys had none at all about accepting it, and immediately caught a train to Brighton with 'pulses beating furiously'.

What disturbed his pulses was not the challenge of the work itself but the gender of his pupils. He saw them as 'schools' of girls, not in the obvious sense but as 'gleaming porpoises; shoals and shoals of them, waiting for their new professor at West Brighton'. Although by now in his early twenties, Powys's sexual fantasies had not fundamentally altered since his Sherborne schooldays, when he would cut alluring sketches of long-limbed women out of the magazine *Ally Sloper* and carry them around in his pocket. Almost certainly still a virgin, he was excited not so much by women as they actually existed as by creatures of his imagination which were a kind of mythical third sex: 'a sort of fleeting, floating, fluttering fantasy of femininity, a kind of Platonic essence of sylph-hood.' A vast gulf separated these visions of loveliness from flesh-and-blood women, who aroused in him fear and even repugnance. This period of his life is probably the most puzzling of his entire existence, the puzzle resting in the difficulty of deducing his true state of mind. Powys himself claims to have been closer to insanity then than at any other time, but since he was inclined to over-statement and self-dramatisation it is hard to know whether or not to accept this at face value. It depends, perhaps, on one's definition of madness. He was certainly prone to neurotic anxieties, forever washing his hands and even asking people to open doors for him lest he be contaminated by contact with the handle; one is irresistibly reminded of the compulsive behaviour of the reclusive millionaire Howard Hughes half a century later. 'I became,' Powys memorably notes, 'a perambulating Pilate.' He also developed an aversion to certain fabrics, especially cotton, flinching from contact with as apparently harmless an object as a tablecloth. 'Handkerchiefs were my abomination, unless they were made of silk. To see a woman hold a handkerchief in her hand was intolerable to me,' he confessed.

A woman (that is, a real-life woman) made the sight so much worse because aspects of femininity were abhorrent to him. His daily walks with his high-bred bitch retriever Thora were ruined when, as he curiously puts it, 'I had occasion ere long ... to realise that the companion of my walks belonged to the feminine sex.'

> A gulf of femininity opened beneath my feet. It made me shudder with a singular revulsion. Everything I looked at in Nature — well can I remember one particular walk when this happened — presented itself to me as a repetition of the feminineness of Thora! I could no longer enjoy the singing of the birds. They might be feminine birds! I loathed the thought that so many of the trees and the flowers possessed feminine organs. The thing went so far with me that I became panic-stricken lest I myself should develop feminine breasts, breasts with nipples, resembling the dugs of Thora. It was unpleasant to me even to encounter the harmless little hedge-flower that my father would never fail to remind me was named 'Nipple-Wort'. For several years — and, mark you, this continued for a long while after my marriage — I used to be at the most careful pains to arrange my knife and fork on my plate so *that they should not point at my breast.*
>
> (*Autobiography*, 223)

His deepest aversion of all was to the sexual act. He wished children might be born from trees, or out of dragon's teeth sown in the earth. When an acquaintance innocently mentioned the seed of man while they were both waiting for a train in Brighton station, he was so violently sick that he had to be revived with brandy. Yet this disgust with the physical realities of sex existed alongside his mania for imaginary sylphs. He would walk the beach at Brighton ogling at figures which to some degree possessed the attributes that gave him such tremulous satisfaction, thrilling especially to the sight of their limbs and ankles.

> So completely cerebral was the whole thing with me, that I remember once on the Brighton front coming to the austere conclusion that it was a purer, higher and nobler thing to make a cult of the beauty of young men rather than that of young women. Vividly can I recall the complete desolation that fell at that moment upon land and sea! The light went out; the air grew chill; and I realised that though no real girls equalled the pictures of them in my mind, life became as grey and sinister and weird, as if under an eclipse of the sun, when the feminine principle was expurgated.
> (*Autobiography*, 221)

It is hard to imagine any young man less temperamentally fitted for marriage than John Cowper Powys, but the fact is that within two years of going to Brighton he took Margaret Alice Lyon, sister of his close college friend Harry Lyon, to the altar. The circumstances of his proposal were as remarkable as anything in his often bizarre life. Far from putting the question in the romantic setting of Devon moorland, as the hitherto accepted version of events has it, he was driven into Margaret's arms by the strictness of his mother's view of the right and proper way for a young Victorian gentleman to behave. In the words of Oliver Marlow Wilkinson, son of Powys's close confidant Louis (Marlow) Wilkinson:

> He [John Cowper Powys] told my father that he had no intention of marrying Margaret. He had simply been seeing her and one night he went back to Montacute. His mother looked at him and knew he'd been meeting her and said, 'Young men must not trifle with young women's affections' and he was horrified. He said he got up at that moment and ran overnight all the way to where she lived, which was miles

away, huddled in the porch till morning and proposed when
the girl came down.

That a couple who had merely been keeping company in a casual way should be precipitated into marriage in this fashion seems extraordinary, and there must have been some attraction beyond mere friendship to account for Margaret's acceptance of his proposal, however thrilled she might have been by his headlong flight to her doorstep. She remains a shadowy figure on the brightly-lit stage of John Cowper Powys's life, remembered as being conventional in her attitudes and formal in her manners, but he initially saw her as something of a child of nature. The poems he wrote in her praise around the time of their marriage make much of her sympathy with the natural world:

Well I remember, O my sweet,
How first beside your native wood
I found you, like a flower complete
In perfect flush of maidenhood,
Above your head the rocks looked down
With mystic meanings in their look;
You loved their smile, you feared their frown,
And read their visage like a book,
The hills were yours to roam at will,
The fragrance of the heath and thyme;
Fragrance of gorse did seem to fill
Your being with the dance of rhyme.
With many a lonely flower and tree
A close companionship you made,
Half guessing at the mystery
That kept them single in the glade.
Wild creatures of the field and wood
Crouched at your feet and knew your call.

This is one of several poems simply entitled 'To M.A.' which appeared in his first two collections of poems, published in the 1890s. They serve to remind us that Powys first saw his destiny as that of a great poet, although he later came to dismiss his early poetry as consisting of mere 'copy-cat verses'. Whatever their literary defects, they have the virtue of throwing light on his feelings for Margaret, whose love of the outdoors is celebrated in another poem in which Powys concludes that

The waywardness of mountain brooks
Are in thy face, and from thine eyes
The very soul of nature looks,
The very spirit of the skies.

It is true that Powys often appears to be straining after poetical effect rather than conveying even a lover's distorted view of the beloved, but there is no reason to suppose him insincere in his admiration for his bride. She appears to have been physically attractive, impressing him especially with her 'soft sad beautiful eyes,' and something of her impatience with the stuffier literary conversations at Montacute is revealed by her heartfelt reaction to one of these: 'O these modern litterateurs! Would I had been born the only tomboy among the ladies of a hundred years ago!'

It was Margaret's misfortune to marry a man whose sexual inhibitions were such that he had great difficulty consummating their marriage, which took place at St Michael's Church, Ilsington, in the county of Devon, on 9 April 1896. At this stage of his life, and perhaps long afterwards, Powys appears to have equated any kind of sexual congress with rape. Llewelyn Powys once declared himself 'revolted' by his brother's preference for sex without penetration, drawing from him the gentle admonition: 'You make love in your way, and I make love in mine.' John Cowper Powys appears to have been especially averse to copulating with a virgin, which led to difficulties resolved only when Margaret underwent a minor operation for the piercing of her hymen. The fact that she eventually conceived and gave birth to their only child Littleton Alfred in 1902 was to be a source of wonder to him forever afterwards. Powys's problems in relation to 'normal' sex inevitably make one wonder if he was, in fact, homosexual. He writes unashamedly about the beauty of some of the boys who were with him at Sherborne, but his admiration appears not to have found physical expression. Engagingly, he tells us in his *Autobiography* that his belief in a flaming Hell for wilful sensualists 'never prevented me from indulging my attraction to beautiful boys as long as I did not actually embrace them'. More specifically, writing to his correspondent Glyn Hughes in 1957, he confessed that he had 'once tried so hard' to be 'a homo' but

> I found it impossible to be a 'homo' in this quaint modern sense about which it is now the fashion to talk! No, I found that I was hopelessly attracted to the opposite sex but in such

> funny ways!
>
> I have a *horror* of 'fucking' as it is called. It is amazing how I ever managed to have a son! But I did *somehow* and he was the best friend or the most dearly loved friend I've ever had!
>
> (PTGH, 26)

To seek real-life inspiration for fictional characters is often an arid exercise, but there are those who maintain that the young beauty Gerda, who marries the protagonist in *Wolf Solent*, is modelled on Margaret. If so, it is a Margaret who has so far not been revealed to us, for Gerda has an 'innocent wantonness' which allows her to be photographed 'mounted astride of a girt tombstone'. More endearingly, she is able to imitate a blackbird's song to perfection.

> The girl was not the particular physical type that appealed to him most, or that had, whenever he had come across it, the most provocative effect upon his senses; but the effect upon him of a beauty so overpowering, so absolute in its flawlessness, was great enough to sweep out of sight all previous predilections. And now, as he conjured up the vision of what she was like, it seemed that nothing more desirable could possibly happen to him than to enjoy such beauty.
>
> (WoS, 61)

Gerda is no peeled willow-wand, for she possesses rounded and voluptuous limbs, 'just as her face had something of that lethargic sulkiness that is seen sometimes in ancient Greek sculpture'. For all her impetuosity and unconscious eroticism, Gerda is at heart conventional, seeking in her husband a stability which Wolf fails to provide. It is in her marital unhappiness that we can best see resemblances to Margaret, who like Gerda found herself saddled with a husband unable to construct a way of life which would provide her with a comfortable routine and a steady income. It would be a peculiarly brutal revenge that Powys exacted on her shortcomings if he consciously modelled Gerda on her, since with her rigid class consciousness she would scarcely have welcomed her fictional incarnation as the daughter of a stonemason.

Five

John Cowper Powys and his bride began their married life at Court House near Offham, a Sussex village on the fringe of the South Downs near Lewes. It had historical associations, for it was reputedly built where King Henry III had held court after the Battle of Lewes. Powys rented it for £40 a year, and once again he was the recipient of paternal favours: the Rev Charles Francis Powys increased his annual allowance to £100 and provided £200 for furniture. For a short while before the marriage John Cowper lived a comfortable bachelor life there thanks to the solicitous attention of a housekeeper, the widowed Mrs Curme, whose husband had been the Powyses' gardener at Rothesay House in Dorchester. She was the subject of one of Powys's more humorous anecdotes, for he recalled how one evening, while taking his meal in the kitchen, he offered to read her some poetry. He then launched into Swinburne, giving full weight to such infidel rhetoric as: 'Thou has conquered, O pale Galilean, the world has grown grey with thy breath!'

Mrs Curme's response was unexpected. 'I do thank 'ee, Mr John, from my poor heart,' says she. 'It does me good to hear the dear Lord's name mentioned so frequent!'

Marriage must have come as a shock to the nerves of this strange young man, so thin-skinned and phobia-ridden. We can only guess at his response to his failure to bring his wife sexual fulfilment, but something of his feelings must surely have been projected into those of Dud No-Man, the hero of his novel *Maiden Castle*.

> It was not that he had ever loved her ... with a normal love, for it was Dud's misfortune to be rendered nervously incapable of consummating his marriage, but his bride's startling beauty and singular character had made a deeper impression upon him than anything in his life; and for all these ten years Mona's personality had stood between him and all other

> emotional impressions. Now that it was too late, now that she had died a virgin, the vision of that beautiful body, ready to yield itself and yet so terrifyingly immaculate, had come to absorb every amorous instinct he possessed.
> (MC, 20)

It is possible to see the death of No-Man's wife as symbolising the virtual death of the marriage of John Cowper Powys and Margaret Alice Lyon, which remained a marriage in name only for most of its fifty-three years' existence. After their first decade of uneasy life together Powys was away from home much of his time, lecturing first around England and then in America, and when he settled down permanently with Phyllis Playter as his companion the separation was complete.

Marriage to Margaret did not cure Powys of his mania for scouring Brighton for the sight of shapely limbs and ankles. He likened his desperate search for these to the hopeless addiction of a drug addict. He would make any excuse to get away, running down the slopes of hills while imagining himself 'on the way to some incredible paradise of sylphs'. Yet he knew in his heart, and wryly confessed it in *Autobiography*, that he could not have put up with the personalities of the women who owned those exquisite ankles for half a day.

There were other pleasures to be obtained in Brighton. He loved the seafront, with its sweet-sellers and purveyors of cockles and mussels and winkles, the black-faced minstrels, the Punch-and-Judy shows and street preachers. In the brazen sunshine of memory he would recall how the smells of seaweed and fish and tar and rope had mingled with those of cheap perfumes and 'foam-drenched petticoats' to produce a heady concoction. He remembered, too, how as a young bachelor he had enjoyed the four-mile walk into town from Southwick, where he rented an upstairs room overlooking the sea from the amiable grocer Mr Pollard. His working life, however, continued much the same after marriage as before. He still lectured to his shoals of girls, though no doubt they were less porpoise-slippery in their demure school uniforms than they had been in his imagination. It was a testing routine involving morning and afternoon sessions at different schools, sustained only by a light lunch of boiled eggs, tea and bread and butter: the stomach ulcers which were a lifelong curse were by this time severely restricting his diet.

Powys's marriage introduced him to people who became boon

companions. One of these was Bernard Price O'Neill, whom he described with typical flattery as a 'man of unique genius' with a mixture of Irish and Welsh blood. O'Neill was a physician whose humorous commentaries on life appealed strongly not only to John Cowper but to the Powys family as a whole, supplying them 'with overtones and undertones drawn from the erudition we suspected, the popular slang we avoided, the art we despised.' Another influence at the time was John William Williams, a scholarly man who became known in Powys circles simply as 'The Catholic'. Having been brought up to suspect all Catholics, whom his father considered to be in close conspiracy with the Devil, Powys was surprised to find in him a deep-rooted wisdom he valued. At this time Powys was being drawn towards Roman Catholicism because of his need for 'something with a real tradition behind it, where the myths I loved, and the ballad-poetry I loved, went down deep into the soil of history.' The tendency was encouraged by his growing bond with his brother-in-law, Harry Lyon, a convert to Anglo-Catholicism. His deepest friendship, however, was with Louis (Marlow) Wilkinson, who became for Powys both confidant and irritant, a man who in spite of satirising him mercilessly in his novel *The Buffoon* retained his regard and trust to the end.

Wilkinson was, in Powys's eyes, a 'resplendent personage'. Standing well over six feet tall, he had a devil-may-care attitude to life which sharply contrasted with Powys's old-maidish fastidiousness. He was introduced to the Powys circle by John Cowper's brother Theodore, who had been sent to the small school in Aldeburgh run by Wilkinson's father. It was Theodore who dubbed Wilkinson 'The Archangel,' a name that stuck even after Wilkinson's expulsion from Oxford for blasphemy. With typical insouciance Wilkinson simply transferred to Cambridge, where he was a close friend of yet another Powys brother, Llewelyn. From the start, John Cowper had an ambivalent attitude towards him:

> As for me I felt sometimes affectionate to him, sometimes jealous of him, but always so completely different from him that I would soon lose interest in any attempt to justify myself. The more strongly did he express his opinion of my mental and spiritual trickery, pointing out that I was betraying all the hardly-won values of the life of reason, the more my masochistic and malicious humility would lead him on to misunderstand me and lambast me further and further. At such time he

> resembled a great healthy-natured male unicorn, in the midst of a garden of fragrant white roses, who suddenly shows by his tossings and tramplings and rearings that a serpent has got through the picket-fence.
> (*Autobiography*, 268)

The stimulating company of such men did much to ease the discomfort of marriage to an unsuitable partner, and more distraction came in the form of a fresh occupation. In 1898 John Cowper Powys exchanged the claustrophobic circle of girls' schools in Brighton for the broad acres of England by becoming a university extension lecturer, travelling far and wide to deliver lectures on English literature. This was a job requiring not only knowledge of an eclectic kind but immense stamina, for one tour of duty began in Newcastle-on-Tyne and ended in the Sussex town of Lewes more than a week later. In the context of his achievements as a novelist and essayist it is easy to dismiss these ten years of almost constant travel as unimportant, especially as he maintained that the people he met passed almost entirely out of his mind. Since the work entailed staying overnight in private houses, however, experiencing — albeit briefly — all kinds of English family life, he would have absorbed impressions of people and situations which must surely have enriched his imagination. He certainly enriched the lives of those who heard him, as a letter he received long afterwards from a Mrs Grace E.S. Townsend proves. She recalls writing essays for him as a girl of sixteen, travelling three and a half miles from a country vicarage to hear him lecture in Rochdale.

> A great audience gathered & then you came on the platform looking like my naughty sister said like a farmer's boy. You began and your face lit up & changed completely and we were all held. I was Thrilled by it and writing the Essays was the joy of my life ...
>
> I have always been so grateful for your Lectures — they opened up a new world to me. My sisters still teaze [sic] me about one remark you put on an essay. 'I hate this phrase intellectual treat — please please avoid.' I was greatly distressed by that but as a rule you were very encouraging to me.
> (PSN no 20, 30)

The magic was still potent after more than forty years, for the letter is dated May 25th, 1948.

From being a tyro lecturer in Brighton, Powys thus embarked seriously on a career which was to provide him with a living for nearly four decades. His style was so unusual that it encouraged his academic critics, always numerous, to describe him as a charlatan, a word he joyfully embraced. The fact that he spoke entirely without notes was not in itself a strikingly unusual accomplishment; what raised his performances far above the commonplace was his unique ability to *empathise* with the subject of his lecture. By some extraordinary process of identification, akin to osmosis of the spirit, he *became* the person he was talking about.

> Such was my young-girl-like receptivity that just as Wordsworth's young women give themselves up to the elements so I gave myself up to the spirit of my particular man of genius. And it was with an almost erotic emotion, as if I were indulging myself in some kind of perverted love affair, that I entered the nerves of Dickens or Paul Verlaine or Henry James or Dostoievsky or Keats or Blake! .... What I aimed at was a sort of transmigration of my soul, till, like a demon possessing a person, I serpentined myself into the skeleton of my author, and expounded his most eccentric reactions to life from the actual nerve-centres where these reactions originated.
> (*Autobiography*, 457)

Those unsympathetic to Powys will find it easy to dismiss this remarkable claim as yet another example of his weakness for self-dramatisation, yet there is abundant evidence that when he stepped on to a platform amazing things happened. In a short space of time he was transformed, even transmogrified, by his genius for assimilation into the personality of a long-dead author or a fictional character. Benson Roberts, the erudite Bridgend grocer who persuaded him to lecture in South Wales in the 1930s, noted 'the mesmeric effect of his incantatory declamation'. The magic was still potent in the war years of the 1940s, when he gave a lecture on *King Lear* to the English Society at the University College of Wales, Aberystwyth. More than forty years later its electric effect on a by no means uncritical audience remained clear in the mind of the eminent author and scholar Gwyn Jones, in a conversation with the writer of this biography:

> It was an amazing performance, and I can't think that anybody else could do it so splendidly, so flamboyantly and yet with tremendous feeling, and achieve such striking effects ....

> He was possessed by the work as though some magic transfusion of King Lear into John Cowper Powys had taken place, and he spoke with passion and feeling about the old man, about his daughters, about fate, about human misery, about triumph, about reconciliation, all this .... He was a tall and very notable figure with a wonderful head, a fine voice .... The one moment I remember, and I would think everybody who heard this remembers, was when he stepped forward and braced himself on his right foot predominantly, and raised his right hand in the air, clenched his fingers and described *King Lear* as 'one whole vast symphony of pain'. This was one of the most impressive sentences I ever heard, and I think that was true of all the audience.

Gwyn Jones recalled Powys's gestures that day as being those of an actor, adding 'but with him they never appeared to be the gestures of an actor; they were innate.' This observation supports Powys's claim that his thespian skills were not acquired but instinctive. As a very young child he had acted the part of his father in the Shirley pulpit, although he had no conscious memory of seeing him in it. Later he took on the role of general in the Volentia Army in Dorchester, then — 'the easiest of all roles for me' — of a madman at Wildman's House in Sherborne. At Corpus he was the Boswellian disciple of learned people he chose to call his gurus, and in America he became 'a mixture of a comic Dan Leno and a prophetic Savanarola', calling up spirits like Shakespeare's Glendower. He thought of himself as one possessed, inventing a great new art.

> By getting rid of all 'high-brow' solemnity, of all academic 'correctness' and 'documentation,' under the Rabelaisian encouragement of my unique circus-manager, I succeeded eventually in *hollowing myself out*, like an elder-stalk with the sap removed, so that my whole personality, every least movement I made, and every flicker, wrinkle, and quiver of my face, became expressive of the particular subject I was interpreting.
>
> (*Autobiography*, 449)

The time he spent as a university extension lecturer must have played no small part in preparing Powys for the intellectual and physical challenge of America, which was to come later. His success was such that he was taken on by Cambridge and London universities as well as by Oxford. In his account of these years, Derek Langridge reproduces the detailed syllabus of a course of twelve lectures which Powys gave on 'Representative Prose Writers of the Nineteenth Century' (AROA, 23). This shows that Powys gave two lectures apiece on Charles Lamb, Thomas Carlyle and Walter Pater and single lectures on De Quincey, Hazlitt, Landor, Macaulay, Ruskin and Newman. The accompanying notes are revealing not only of their subjects' felicity of phrase but of John Cowper Powys's. He notes that Lamb was a master of 'melting his soul into speech,' that De Quincey's imagination 'fuses the Beautiful and the Repulsive in enforced nuptials,' that Hazlitt's childhood, youth and early manhood 'are so many idols which he worships with the smoke of unextinguished altars', and (perhaps most strikingly of all) that Newman's style is so chaste and exact that, sculptor-like, 'we see the chips flying from the marble'.

By the time these lectures were delivered in north-east England in the Lent term of 1903, the Powyses had moved house and John Cowper, to his eternal amazement, had become a father. Feeling shut off from the sunshine at Court House, in its fold of the South Downs, they opted for Bankside in Burpham, not far from Arundel. This time Charles Francis Powys's purse remained buttoned-up, for he disapproved of the move, but with the help of the parish priest at Burpham his son and heir managed to buy the house on a 999-year lease for £500. There were difficulties with the locals, for Powys became increasingly vexed with the village children's habit of using the prehistoric embankment overlooking his small garden as a playground. He placed a gigantic board inscribed 'Trespassers Will Be Prosecuted' on top of the earthwork, but it was soon thrown into the ditch by indignant villagers. Some time later Powys observed a dark-bearded figure surveying the scene curiously; it turned out to be the owner of the embankment, none other than the first in rank of all English peers, the Duke of Norfolk.

It was at Burpham, after the birth of his son Littleton Alfred in August 1902, that John Cowper Powys suddenly acquired a passion for everything Welsh.

> I bought Welsh grammars, Welsh dictionaries, Welsh modern poetry. I bought an elaborate Welsh Genealogy, called 'Powys-Fadoc,' and mightily chagrined was I when I found no mention of my father's ancestors in it! I bought everything

> I could lay my hands on that had to do with Wales and with the Welsh people. Alas! I had not learnt yet ... that Providence had deprived me of the least tincture of philology. I soon gave up trying to learn Welsh. But the *idea* of Wales and the *idea* of Welsh mythology went drumming on like an incantation through my tantalised soul.
> (*Autobiography*, 332)

He even thought of selling up and wandering off with his family and his folios 'to some remote hiding-place in Mid-Wales' but decided against it because 'the older my son grew the more impossible of realisation became this wild dream.' One also suspects that his wife would have had something to say about it. Wild dreams, however, have a habit of surviving if they are strong enough and this one would eventually find fulfilment thirty years later; though the woman destined to go with him to Wales was not Margaret.

Six

Critics generally have been as dismissive of John Cowper Powys's first two collections of verse (*Odes and Other Poems*, 1896, and *Poems*, 1899) as he was himself. Imitative though they were, however, they have their moments. 'Song of the North Wind' in *Odes* has a relentless rhythm and energy:

> Fanned by my breath cometh rumour of battle,
> and madness of peoples,
> Hearts that are heavy with hate, hands that
> are clenched for a crime;
> Baffled and brimmed by my fury, earth's rivers
> are reeds to be riven;
> Pillaged and pierced by my wrath, cornfields
> are chaff to be strewn.

There are obvious echoes of Swinburne and Meredith in these early poems, and one of his heroes, Keats, is celebrated in a style so archaic as to be almost a parody:

> I wept the fading of the Olympian dawn,
> Shapes so divine turned to an empty name,
> Until to ease my fond lamenting came
> Thy flowery car on summer winds upborne ...

If Powys had been a poor boy scribbling away in a cottage it is highly unlikely that such efforts would have been rewarded with publication by William Rider & Sons. This London firm, however, had Ralph Shirley as a partner, and Shirley happened to be a cousin of John Cowper Powys. The Rev Charles Francis Powys dipped into his pocket to meet the cost of publication, so with a gale force of nepotism behind it this handsomely-produced collection duly appeared in the bookshops. It was followed three years later by

Poems, thanks again to the influence of Shirley and subsidy from C.F. Powys.

For all his professions of being a clown and a zany, John Cowper Powys always had an eye for the main chance. There is something discomfiting about poems dedicated not only to Olympians such as Keats and Cowper but eminent contemporaries like Hardy and Yeats. Was this simple admiration or literary toadyism? The poet and critic Roland Mathias, in a penetrating study of the poetry of John Cowper Powys, writes:

> One may indeed reflect ... not merely on the ease with which a young man (or a young man with the right contacts) could get his poetry published in 1896 — both publishers' attitudes and the degree of competition being so much more demanding in the present — but also upon the manner in which both Yeats and Hardy came to know of the contents of this slim gold-and-apple-green volume. It all depends, does it not, on how much is to be allotted to 'propitiation' (a word JCP uses to cover his advances to individuals both after a contretemps and at a first meeting) and how much to forwarding of career?
> (THOES, 29)

Powys's own awareness of his deficiencies as a poet did not in any way diminish the sense of destiny he had possessed ever since, as a child, he had seen himself as a magician and 'the Lord of Hosts'.

> Yes, I knew I was a mere imitating copy-cat, repeating, repeating, repeating the rhythms of men of genius. But ... I knew then, just as I knew twenty years later, when I had not published anything else, that I *was*, in some way impossible to prove, a great and for all my cringings and propitiations a terrifyingly formidable genius!
> (*Autobiography*, 225)

For all his faith in himself, there is evidence of a growing sense of frustration in his remark to his brother Llewelyn in 1905: 'Thirty-three, the age when our Lord was crucified, and I've written nothing but a few poems and a chapter or two of a bawdy novel.' By then, however, he had undergone experiences which would provide material for him as a novelist many years later. Some of these were the result of his curious friendship with Tom Jones, a Liverpool shipping clerk who had little in common with the Burpham circle.

A Welshman, short in stature and with a limp, Jones had a formidable personality which women found attractive. Through him Powys enjoyed occasions of sensual indulgence which, in his case at any rate, appear to have fallen short of full sexual congress. He describes them as being 'purely and simply, friendly erotic encounters between men and women,' with no bitter after-taste of guilt or responsibility. Intensely class-conscious, he was not quite sure if these 'sweet-natured women' belonged to the lower-middle-class or the proletariat, or even whether or not they were Welsh like Tom Jones; one would have thought that their accents at least might have revealed this. They gave him, however, delicious experiences which he likened to 'Arcadias of idyllic felicity'. Jones and Powys were joined in some of these adventures by Louis (Marlow) Wilkinson, who in his novel *The Buffoon* (in which he appears as Edward, Jones as Fielding and Powys is thinly disguised as Jack Welsh) mercilessly parodies one of these sessions:

> The children of nature arrived, one by one, between eight and nine. Ethelle came first, in a huge picture-hat and a bright yellow blouse. She was painted and powdered, — distastefully meretricious to Fielding, Edward felt. The girl immediately displayed the greatest devotion to Welsh: she sat on a foot-stool by his chair, and played tenderly with his abnormal worsted socks. Repeatedly she addressed him as 'dear 'eart'; her voice seemed to tremble with genuine emotion ...
>
> Welsh's aspect, as Edward looked, was difficult to interpret. His eyes were keen and bright and fixed, as though preoccupied with some distant object, the visualising of which demanded extreme concentration: his mouth, on the other hand, was lax and dropped, — vacuous, as though all energies had been apathetically dismissed. One of his hands rested tentatively just above the girl's knee, which he kept pressing gently in a queer mechanical way; the other hand held a thin strand of her yellow hair, twisting and untwisting it with a slow and regular motion of its hard knotted fingers.
>
> (TB, 243)

It was around this time that Powys met 'a little street-girl called Lily', with whom he struck up a friendship which must have had at least some degree of intimacy about it, as he revealed that she had shocked him when she first took off her clothes by the way she had padded herself, especially around the hips, in order to look plumper than she actually was. Richard Perceval Graves notes that Margaret even allowed her to visit them at Burpham, 'perhaps believing that John was trying to reclaim Lily from her life of sin; but the visit was not a success: one of the servants, realising Lily's profession, was so outraged that she would not wait upon her' (TBP, 55).

Such diversions eased the burden of lecturing which won Powys so high a reputation that he was invited to lecture in Bremen, Hamburg and Dresden in the first decade of the twentieth century. It was the USA, however, which was to make of him virtually an expatriate for many years, his first visit in the winter of 1904-05 being the result of an invitation from the American Society for the Extension of University Teaching. He sailed from Liverpool on the Cunard liner *Ivernia* on 24 December 1904 (Tom Jones seeing him off at the dockside), to arrive in New York on 3 January 1905, the day after the official opening of the Times Building. He was immediately struck by the liveliness of the scene, telling his mother in a letter home of the 'many extraordinary things' he had witnessed.

> The Peoples [sic] Institute lecture in New York was remarkable. Down in a crypt supported by pillars — like a catacomb — a large audience of Italians, Germans, Socialists, Anarchists, Democrats, Men gesticulating, asking wild questions, disputing with each other, shouting, cursing the corruption of the government and the exploiting of the poor by the rich — haranguing, howling like revolutionary incendiaries ... 'Tell me Professor!' one would yell 'The Greeks and Jews — were they ever, if you go far back, the same race?' 'Professor!' another would cry — 'Is the Goddess Demeter and the Catholic Madonna the same person?'
> (PSN, July 1992, 12)

On the voyage out he had wondered what wisdom he might find to impart, concluding rather dispiritingly that he was devoid of any conviction in religion, morality, politics or indeed anything else. This was a theme he would develop in *Confessions of Two Brothers*, written in association with Llewelyn Powys and published in 1916, in which he maintained that 'I have no Philosophy; not even the Philosophy of having no Philosophy ... I doubt even the validity of doubt'. The nihilism of this sits oddly with what we know of John Cowper Powys as the upholder of a philosophy of life which many have found satisfactory and even inspiring, but such musings on his own deficiencies should not be taken too seriously. Long before he set foot in America he had become convinced of the immorality of vivisection, and although not a practising Christian (his faltering steps towards Catholicism having stopped a good way short of Rome) he sometimes spoke of God with an easy familiarity that would have pleased his father. Thus in a letter to his brother Llewelyn from the Lake District town of Keswick in 1902:

> There are many and various degrees of 'dissent' and 'assent' to Christianity. Christ appears sometimes as a god sometimes as a half-god, sometimes as a Prophet sometimes as a great Genius — and sometimes as an attractive but dangerous Revolutionary. It is possible also to take the main secrets of his doctrine on their human side and omit altogether the supernatural; it is also possible to regard all men as Incarnations of God and Him — (the wisest and best) the fullest Incarnation .... For myself it is enough for me, as I thought within myself rowing upon the lake surrounded by the mighty mountains, to feel below my human will and below all material forms of Nature one great eternal Spirit in whom we live and move and have our being — God is everything and everything is God and true worship is that ecstasy wherein we forget ourselves and are able to live in the great tides of feeling which roll through all animate and inanimate nature.
> (LTHBL, Vol 1, 17)

The closeness of the bond with Llewelyn produced a correspondence which throws much light on John Cowper Powys's state of mind from around the time of his thirtieth birthday. These letters, invariably addressed to 'Lulu' with varying degrees of affection, show that in spite of the marital difficulties he felt concern for his wife and, increasingly, remorse over his gradual estrangement from her. Soon after the move to Burpham he notes with pleasure that she finds the local people friendly, so that he at least has the satisfaction of knowing that when he is away lecturing that winter 'I shall feel she is well looked after and happy'. By the end of the decade, however, he is given to self-laceration over his treatment of her:

> When you destroy a life-illusion you commit the one unpardonable sin. I have done it — I cannot be forgiven — I destroyed my wife's illusion of 'love'.
> (ibid, 86)

His financial support for Margaret was, however, to be unstinting, even when his own finances were shaky. He would, in fact, show heroic loyalty in his determination that his wife and son should suffer as little as possible from the hazards of the way of life he had adopted.

Perhaps the most interesting revelation in the correspondence, however, is the depth of his feeling for Llewelyn, whom he addresses in terms of endearment which families less given to such hot-house affinities would find strange, even embarrassing. 'My dearest Lulu' or 'My Lulu' becomes 'My darling' when Llewelyn is lying in a Swiss sanatorium stricken with TB, the recipient of letters of feverish abandon.

> Never have I known how I loved you till now. I see your old dear rugged forehead, I see your unequalled mouth — I fancy the most sensitive mouth that ever has been made and so soft and gentle ... I tell you, dear, if you recover it will be the greatest Happiness of my life — O by far the greatest! So you must *will* get well? Who knows? I shall kiss you. O I shall kiss like a lover as I do now in soul — O my love — JACK XXXXXXXXXXXXXXXXXXXXXXXXX
> (ibid, 57)

These are not the terms in which brothers usually express their affection, even when one of them has a potentially fatal illness. It is all part of that intensity of feeling and tribal exclusiveness upon which people like Louis Wilkinson have remarked. In his uninhibited outpourings John Cowper Powys was profoundly un-English, a trait which he might joyfully have admitted in support of his claim to be a Welsh aboriginal. He was unashamed in his affection for and even adoration of the brother twelve years his junior who as a small boy appeared to him like 'the angel that John saw in the Sun'. Later he became, for John Cowper, a 'champion of natural joy', possessing a 'warm, sun-born, earth-rooted nature' which contrasted with his own 'cold planetary heart'. Llewelyn, for his part, had from an early age seen his eldest brother almost as a father-figure, calling him Daddy Jack and watching him with a 'puzzled earnestness' as he read a book in the Montacute drawing-room, as if anxious to learn the secret of his absorption. In some ways Daddy Jack undeniably took on a fatherly role, responding compassionately when Lulu, then a Sherborne schoolboy, turned to him for advice he could seek from no-one else during a personal crisis. Llewelyn was forever grateful, exclaiming when someone accused him of suffering from a brother complex: 'Have I not for a quarter of a century followed in the wake of John Cowper? All that I am I owe to him.'

Llewelyn, a man of strongly independent cast of mind not given to idolatry, spoke of himself as a 'sagacious Sancho Panza' following his brother closely, and the equally iconoclastic Louis Wilkinson went so far as to liken the appearance of the young John Cowper Powys to that of a young god, 'hard-fleshed, keen-boned, lean-bellied.' He remarked on the high tone of his 'Red Indian' cheeks, which almost appeared to be artificially coloured. This was the man who made such a profound impression on the American audiences he faced as a touring lecturer, a kind of intellectual showman who pulled out all the stops to uplift and entrance them. He was distrusted and often despised by academia but for people with no intellectual pretensions he was like a prophet. He spoke, wrote the actor/director Maurice Browne, 'like a trumpet calling to battle'.

The American Society for the Extension of University Teaching, based in Philadelphia, arranged all of Powys's early lecture tours of the USA. He combined them with his university extension teaching in Britain until 1910, when he completely transferred his lecturing work across the Atlantic and henceforth spent the greater part of each year in the States. Crucial to this decision was the setting up of the University Lecturers' Association of New York, a rival organisation to the Philadelphia-based ASEUT. Louis Wilkinson, by then an established figure on the American lecture circuit himself, played a leading role in creating the new body in association with G. Arnold Shaw, a go-ahead young Englishman whom Powys had met on his first voyage to the States in 1904-05. After a row with the ASEUT over fees, Wilkinson asked Shaw to arrange his lectures for him, and Powys enthusiastically joined them in forming the ULANW. 'I think it will really work out — I hope so,' he told Llewelyn.

Originally based at 11 Charles Street in New York, the association was a success, and not only financially. Powys immediately struck up a close friendship with Shaw, although in many ways they appear to have been exact opposites: Shaw was a cigar-smoking extrovert who loved to fill his stomach with steak and onions and to spice his conversation with the latest slang. They were alike, however, in their attitude to the lecture tours which Shaw arranged for twenty per cent commission. They believed the lectures should rank as public entertainment rather than being mere 'cultural stunts'. They were akin, too, in their dislike of moral pomposity and what Powys termed 'patronizing intellectualism'.

> We were in fact — lecturer and manager — what people call 'a fair pair'. I was the clown of our circus, and Arnold was the ringmaster, the fellow with the smooth forehead, the bland smile, and the long whip. How roguishly he would crack this whip when his poor Cagliostro was despatched on a tour half across the Continent!
>
> '*A mean jump* for you, John!' he would say with a chuckle. (*Autobiography*, 447)

The American phase of John Cowper Powys's life, which lasted more than a quarter of a century, was an odyssey of Homeric proportions during which he would often travel hundreds of miles each way for a single lecture, staying in hotel rooms as infinite in their variety as the American people themselves. He lectured mostly on individual writers and their works, Shaw publicising his forthcoming appearances with imaginative flair. He spoke in 'remote little radical halls' and in theatres and institutes, to members of clubs and associations or to the general public, to anyone, in fact, who would listen. Once he spoke for more than two hours on Thomas Hardy to an audience of two thousand in Chicago and at the end the audience rose to their feet, demanding more. Those who liked him best, he would say, were Jews, communists and Catholics, because 'all these three are in essence *intensely religious*, for even the doctrinal atheism and official materialism of Communist theory have most strangely to do with the controlling religious nerve.'

In the end it all became too much for him, but perhaps it was America which made him, for it was amid what he called the 'wild, free, boundless *chaos* of it all' that he got down to his life's work of writing the long romantic novels which for years he had felt destined to write. Remarkably, it was on those marathon train journeys through America, from one lecture to another, that he was able to evoke the very essence of the English landscape in such novels as *Wolf Solent*; yet perhaps the distance itself provided the necessary perspective. For the fictional world Powys created in these novels was not the England that actually existed in the late 1920s and early 1930s, but a strange mixture of the Victorian England of his youth and an imagined present. America, the great melting pot, was for him a crucible as magical as any to be found in the kind of mythology he treasured.

Seven

In January 1912, when in his fortieth year, John Cowper Powys met a woman who in some ways was as extraordinary as himself. She was Frances Gregg, a young American who moved in exalted literary circles. Some years earlier she had fallen in love with Ezra Pound, though had never been his lover. She was, in fact, innocent in sexual matters in a way that later generations of young women were never allowed to be. Her best friend was the poet Hilda Doolittle, who had also fallen for Pound and had enjoyed for a while the ambiguous relationship of being 'unofficially engaged'. Both Frances and Hilda belonged to the group of young poets which Pound had gathered around him, progressive in their views and relentless in their pursuit of the artistic life.

Frances approached Powys after one of his lectures in Philadelphia and gave him a poem of hers called 'Perche' — this being the Italian word for 'Because' (although at first he imagined it referred either to a bird's perch or to a fish). Enigmatic and haunting, it immediately struck a chord:

> I am the possessor and the possessed.
> I am of the unborn.
> My kind have not yet come upon the earth.
> *Or — are they gone?*
> Am I then left, a memory of the dead?
> Am I a dram-wraith, a ghost of beauty fled?
> I who possess and am possessed.
>
> Strange madness beset me.
> Passing pageant-wise across my web of thought.
> The red circlet of Narcissus gems my blood —
> And I brood on a golden reed.
> Who doth possess me — I possess.
> *Yea, I am dead!*

In the pale light from the grave
The Sisters weave:
Crimson — and green and golden thread
Upon Time's robe.

Oliver Marlow Wilkinson tells how Powys asked to see more of her work, receiving as a result an invitation to tea with her widowed mother, Mrs Julia Vanness Gregg. Seriously misjudging the formidable Mrs Gregg, he wrote her a letter full of 'the sweet, bland condescension of the great man' (JAF, vol 1, xvi).

It was a mistake he never made again. Julia Vanness Gregg was, in Wilkinson's words, 'a squarish woman built to last for ever'. Her mother, Gertrude Heartt, came from a long line of pioneering women and had campaigned for women's rights in the 1860s; Julia herself would take up cliff climbing in her seventies, roped to her daughter Frances and Frances's children. In John Cowper's (Jack's) correspondence she became 'Madonna,' a figure always to be respected.

Frances, on the other hand, was a figure to be worshipped. Within a few weeks of their first meeting he was writing her passionate letters while on his travels, calling her a 'mad solitary sea-cat,' swearing he would not 'touch with the tips of my fingers a single human being till I see Frances again,' and confessing:

> I tell you I wish I could wash my spotted memory clear of every single sexual emotion I have ever had — except for you; (and I'm damned if that word describes anything *we* ever feel) as you would wash mouth, eyes, throat and every pore of my skin with biting saturnian soap!
> (ibid, 3)

Had Jack and Frances been different kinds of people, living in different times, they might happily have leapt into bed, but instead their liaison never got beyond the despised Lawrentian notion of 'sex in the head'. Interviewed by the present author for a television drama-documentary, Oliver Marlow Wilkinson observed:

> She was a most strange person for him to meet, ideal in a way because she had no knowledge of sex — her mother did not think it right for any girl, and she was then twenty-six — and no knowledge of Englishmen, so she thought him a typical Englishman. So when he made faces at people in the tram she thought it was an English habit. When she asked him why he

> did it he replied 'Because they are making faces at me' which they weren't at all. He confessed his terrible sadism to her, he thought he was a devil .... She thought, what a waste, this man thinks he's evil, he's absorbed in these horrible nightmares, pornographic to a degree, and she shook it out of him. He was terribly in love with her, but not love in an orthodox way, but she didn't know that.
>
> (TGP)

The intensity of Jack's love for Frances precipitated him into action. He could neither marry her himself, nor tolerate the thought of being entirely separated from her. His answer was to marry her off to his best friend, Louis Wilkinson. Oliver Marlow Wilkinson, son of this marriage, tells how Powys turned matchmaker with phenomenal success.

> I remember my mother saying how he described my father as being magnificent, a god, and then he described this girl Frances Gregg to my father as 'a goddess, my friend, a goddess,' so that before they met they were in love with each other and they married within three weeks.
>
> (ibid)

The haste of his parents' marriage was, he believes, partly explained by the fact that both Powys and Louis Wilkinson were about to sail back to England after their six months' tour of duty as lecturers. (Llewelyn Powys also lectured in the USA for Shaw from time to time.) The marriage of Louis Umfreville Wilkinson and Frances Josefa Gregg, which took place at St Stephen's Church in Philadelphia on 10 April 1912, dealt a blow to James Henderson, a rich young American who was also in love with Frances. With typical insouciance, Louis informed his bride that he did not intend to remain faithful to her, to which she retorted that she expected to be faithful to him (JAF, vol 1, xxviii). More remarkable still was the agreement between all interested parties, including the bride's mother, that the marriage should not be consummated for several months. Jack felt so strongly that this curious undertaking ought to be honoured that he stood guard at night outside Frances's cabin on the Cunard liner *Caronia*. By then his Olympian detachment had given way to intense jealousy and frustration and he confessed his misery in a letter to Julia Vanness Gregg, written aboard the liner four days after the wedding.

> I never have the courage to go to her cabin to say good morning. It would be suitable enough as May [Marian Powys, Jack's sister] is there but I cannot do it. I am nervous and self-distrusting in regard to her. Often when she thinks that I want to be away it is only that I dare not assume that she wants me. It is hard to make her understand this and not very wise in me to try to explain it .... O Madonna, Madonna I could cry sometimes. Well — well — A merry game my friends, a merry game and a mad world.
>
> (ibid, 9)

The friendship of Jack and Frances was to prove a lasting one: far more durable than the marriage of Frances and Louis, which ended in divorce. They continued to correspond after Phyllis Playter had become the new love of his life early in the 1920s, Powys expressing his relief at the fact that Phyllis ('my young woman') accepted without question, 'and with a queer kind of silent respect, all that we remain to each other and our queer funny hold on each other's mind.'

It is no surprise to find that Louis Wilkinson and his bride were accompanied on their honeymoon tour of Europe not merely by one Powys but two, Llewelyn joining the party and falling briefly in love with Frances himself. There was a curious episode in Venice, where they quickly tired of the company of the self-styled Baron Corvo (Frederick Rolfe). In a collection of essays, Wilkinson recalled:

> The end came at the bottom of the Campanile. Corvo asked when our next meeting was to be. 'Tomorrow?' — 'We're engaged, I'm afraid, for tomorrow.' John, the eldest, was our spokesman. 'The day after?' — 'I'm afraid we're engaged then too.' — 'Well, perhaps Thursday?' At that point John lost his nerve. 'We're *engaged*!' he shouted. 'All the time. Up to the hilt. Engaged! *Up to the hilt!*' Corvo turned on his heel with one of the swiftest movements I have ever seen and shot away from us across the Piazza.
>
> (SF, 68)

There was a devil inside John Cowper Powys which, when released, could lead to the infliction of terrible hurt.

By this time, he and his wife Margaret were virtually living separate lives, his visits to Burpham occurring as interludes between lecture tours abroad. To the world, however, they still presented the face of a respectable middle-aged couple with a small retinue of domestic servants including a maid or two, cook and gardener. Since their only child, Littleton Alfred, was away at boarding school for much of the time and Powys in America, one might wonder what all these servants found to do, but for Margaret they were a necessary symbol of her position in society. Her Powys in-laws, however, felt she lived in too grand a style and were less than sympathetic when she ran short of money due to her husband's want of a regular income.

When war broke out in August 1914, Margaret was immediately aware of her duty: it was to persuade others to perform theirs. She posted up a notice in the village shop at Burpham saying 'England expects'. Her husband, showing more compassion, was moved by the sight of village boys 'sitting in their open doors with their heads on their hands wrestling with their consciences.' There was no immediate moral pressure on men over forty such as himself to join the crusade against 'the Boche,' but as the war progressed he felt increasingly uneasy about being a non-combatant. He saw the war as 'one single great cock-pit of suffering, to enter which was brave and noble, and to dodge which was base and ignoble.' Yet he acknowledged that all war was crazy, and this particular war 'not only crazy but mean and revolting,' a means by which cool-headed old and middle-aged men tormented hot-blooded youth.

He continued to lecture in America during the war, the submarine menace making him fearful of returning to England for his usual summer visit in 1916. 'Will the war never be over?' he rhetorically asked Llewelyn in a letter from Ohio. He wondered if the authorities might refuse to allow him to work in America after the war if he refused conscription: 'I would sooner be drilled now than exiled for ever.' One of his secret fears concerned not the possibility of death or injury but the embarrassment of having to ask permission to fall out of line on a march in order to urinate; this brought back uncomfortable memories of similar agonies at Sherborne. Eventually he screwed up the courage to present himself at the British recruiting office in New York, only to be rejected because an X-ray revealed an old scar on one of his lungs, evidence of latent tuberculosis. This would undoubtedly have strengthened his sense of kinship with Llewelyn, who had suffered so severely from TB in 1909-10 that he had been sent for treatment to a Swiss sanatorium. Curiously, the stomach ulcers for which John Cowper Powys had undergone radical surgery in the autumn of 1917 were not themselves seen as disqualifying him for military service. Still plagued by conscience, he sailed for England and was medically examined in Brighton under the new conscription act which put men even older than himself into uniform. He recalled being treated with extraordinary tenderness, even being asked to choose the person with whom he wished to undress, and again that old scarring of the lung saved him from the trenches. By then the war was in its final year, and he was able to satisfy his patriotic impulse by lecturing up and down the country on Britain's war aims.

The war years saw Powys's emergence as a published writer not only of poetry but of novels and essays. No fewer than nine titles came out under his name between 1914 and 1917. They include two collections of poetry, *Wolf's Bane* and *Mandragora*; his first two novels, *Wood and Stone* and *Rodmoor*; a collection of literary essays, *Visions and Revisions*; and *Confessions of Two Brothers*, written in collaboration with Llewelyn Powys. This torrent of creativity undoubtedly sprung from the sense of urgency induced by the Great War, John Cowper remarking in *Confessions* that 'the effect of a few weeks in the trenches would be to make me resolve to spend the rest of my life writing desperately and savagely against time, — writing everything I have it in me to write, — writing ferociously with hardly a breathing-space' (COTB, 143). Even outside the trenches, however, the pace of his writing was ferocious enough. The novels provide the first evidence that Powys was capable of the kind of sustained fictional writing he admired so much in others. They fall far short of his major novels in merit, but provide glimpses of what was to come.

Wood and Stone, published in New York in 1915 by the ever-resourceful G. Arnold Shaw, has the strongly autobiographical slant one expects in a first novel, John Cowper Powys and Llewelyn appearing in the unlikely guise of two stonemasons working the local stone in Nevilton, the fictional Montacute. Fraternal in fiction as well as fact, they are 'a noteworthy pair, though scarcely favourites, either with their fellow-workmen or their manager'. James, the John Cowper Powys figure, is morose and reserved, whereas his younger brother Luke has a sunny and serene spirit and is likened to a Greek god. A large cast of characters includes the unsavoury financier Mortimer Romer, who has bought up the local estates, the young high church clergyman Hugh Clavering and the hermit-like Maurice Quincunx, a distant relation of Mrs Romer who has his allowance snatched away by her bullying husband. Subordinate figures are the

Romer daughter Gladys, her meek Italian companion Lacrima (whom she torments) and the Catholic philosopher John Francis Taxater, a gentleman of independent means. The novel provides great sport for those addicted to the literary game of spotting the originals of fictional characters, Quincunx being something of an amalgam of John Cowper and his gloomy brother Theodore and Taxater a version of John Williams, the scholar known to the Powyses as The Catholic. The story grinds laboriously on through 700 pages, Powys's prose displaying little of the vigour he was to bring to his Wessex novels just over a decade later.

Rodmoor, published only a year later by Shaw, shows a striking advance in technique in its opening pages, for in place of a laborious detailing of place and history we are given immediate psychological insight into the hero, Adrian Sorio. We hear of all the 'morbid sufferings' he has endured in America, his 'unhappy habit of deadly introspection,' his 'aching nostalgia for things less murderously new and raw.' He has suffered nervous collapse, his mental illness taking 'so dangerous, so unlooked for a shape, that it was only by the merest chance he had escaped long incarceration.'

Comparisons with Powys's own fears for his sanity are inevitable, and in Adrian's high-flown philosophising we hear echoes of his creator.

> 'The Spring ... whether I cared to recognise it or not, waved thrilling arms towards me. I felt it ... in the warmth of the sun, in the faces of the wistful shop girls, in the leaves budding against the smoke of the Borough. It had come to me again, and you — you had brought it! It had come to me again, the Eternal Return, the antiphonal world-deep Renewal. It had come, Nance, and all the slums of Rotherhithe and Wapping, and all the chimneys, workshops, wharves and tenements of the banks of this river of yours could not stop the rising of the sap ...'
>
> (*Rodmoor*, 13)

The dialogue, although preposterous, has an energy which at least kindles some interest in the character. The novel is set in East Anglia, which Powys knew from visits to his maternal grandfather, and one of its successes is his invocation of landscape and seascape. Adrian is torn between two women, the amenable but boring Nance and the dangerous Philippa. It is to Philippa that he confides his secret thoughts and she is proud to be the recipient of them. She believes him to be hers — 'hers in the heights and the depths' — and despises the 'whimpering human crowd' that surround them. The melodramatic climax finds the 'brain-sick' Adrian dying at the sea's edge and Philippa tying his corpse to her body before plunging suicidally into the waves. Not for the first or last time in his work, Powys succumbs to absurdity.

Eight

Poetry had moved on since the publication of John Cowper Powys's first two collections in the 1890s, and he had moved with it. *Wolf's Bane* (1916) and *Mandragora* (1917) display none of the archaisms of those earlier works. The language is more direct and the poems often freer in structure, sometimes startlingly so. There is nothing in either *Odes* or *Poems* to prepare us for the poem he entitles 'Compensation'. It begins:

> After all
> There are moments,
> Even for the unhappy,
> When, out of some tiny crevice,
> Some small overlooked chink in the great Wine-Vat,
> The good liquor spurts forth
> Into our mouth.

It is as if Powys, with one giant leap, has spanned a century in his development as a poet. The temptation to imitate, in homage rather than parody, is still there, 'The Clock' and 'The Recruit' (both in *Wolf's Bane*) being distinctly Hardyesque. In the same volume, the eight-line 'After Reading William Blake' explicitly echoes 'Songs of Innocence':

> Those who cut a worm in twain
> With Jesus' blood the roadway stain.
> Those who aside from the harlot turn
> Throw Jesus' heart in the flame to burn.

By this time Powys had no need for such sorties into the reverential, having enough resources of his own. What he lacked, perhaps, was the self-confidence as a poet to explore fully his own potential. For much of the time he is still shackled by old conventions of metre and rhyme which others had discarded. Yet even within the limits he imposes upon himself, he achieves impressive results. There is the strange poem he calls 'The Epiphany of the Mad':

> I am the voice of the outcast things,
> The refuse and the drift.
> What the waves wash up and the rivers spurn
> And the Golgothas of the cities burn,
> For these my song I lift.
>
> I sing in dust; I sing in mire;
> I sing in slag and silt;
> I sing in the reek of the rubble-fire;
> I sing where sewers are spilt;
>
> I sing where the paupers have their graves;
> I sing where abortions lie;
> I sing where the mad-house nettles wave;
> I sing where the hearse goes by.
>
> And all my tune is taught by the Moon;
> For the Moon looks down on all;
> And the song I sing of each outcast thing
> Is a mad Moon-madrigal.

Even here, however, Powys has to over-lard the cake, adding a banal stanza that introduces a winsome note of hope serving only to thin out the atmosphere of brooding melancholy he had created:

> But all my thoughts as I sing this tune
> Are about a little star
> That soon or late, that late or soon,
> The evilest things beneath the moon
> Approach and cleansed are.

It should be noted at this point that the poet in John Cowper Powys had not been idle in the seventeen years separating *Poems* and *Wolf's Bane*, for in 1905 he had written his long poem 'Lucifer', which did not appear in print until 1956. Its championship of the arch-enemy of Christ would have been deeply shocking to his parents. The Rev Charles Francis Powys lived to see his eldest son's emergence as a novelist, but Mary Cowper Powys died just before the outbreak of war in 1914. Since she is said to have hated success, the fact that she was spared the knowledge of her first-born's advance as a writer rates perhaps as a perverse kind of blessing.

While the two novels and two poetry collections clearly rank as the most important works by Powys published during the Great War, the merit of his non-fiction should not be overlooked. *Visions and Revisions* and *Suspended Judgements* provide foretastes of the insight he brought to the assessment of renowned authors in *The Pleasures of Literature* more than twenty years later. Some of the sentiments he expressed in his introduction to the new edition of *Visions and Revisions* in 1955 could equally be applied to himself. He speaks of

> ... the great writer's mysteriously unique life-vision, the life-view which is his instinctive reaction in the face of the delicious and horrible, the enjoyable and intolerable experiences of life on this planet; and which in each particular great writer's case includes the way he uses his senses, the way he eats and drinks, the way he responds to the provocation of sex, the whole character, in fact, of his reaction to his condition as a living man or woman, a living boy or girl, upon this earth, rather than a quadruped, a reptile, an insect, a vegetable, or what we call an Inanimate Thing.
> (VAR, vii)

He recalls that the book's title was 'invented for me' by Maurice Browne, who in 1915 was running the Chicago Little Theatre. What this collection of essays amounts to, in his view, 'is a book-lover's private and special shelf of his favourite books,' the writers including Rabelais ('the great cosmogonic medicine-man of besotted humanity'), Shakespeare, Dickens, Goethe, Dostoievsky, Poe and Whitman. The inclusion of Poe is interesting in that, in the opinion of Roland Mathias, his work influenced the poetry in *Wolf's Bane* and *Mandragora*.

The first edition of *Visions and Revisions* was followed a year later by *One Hundred Best Books*, a slim volume providing a précis of each of these chosen works. The list begins with the *Psalms of David* ('the most pathetic and poignant, as well as the most noble and dignified of all poetic literature') and ends with the *Oxford Book of English Verse*. Between them come expected works such as Homer's *Odyssey* and Voltaire's *Candide* and a surprise or two in the shape of novels by the now almost forgotten Gilbert Cannan and Vincent O'Sullivan. In his preface, Powys admits that his choice is 'frankly subjective,' not one of those selections 'designed to stuff the minds of young persons with an accumulation of "standard learning" calculated to alarm and discourage the boldest.'

Confessions of Two Brothers is in some ways the most interesting of the spate of books Powys produced in the Great War years, as his contribution can be seen as a forerunner of his massive *Autobiography*. The original intention was to include the 'confessions' of all six Powys brothers, but only three showed any interest: John Cowper Powys himself (the originator, with his manager/publisher Shaw, of what he calls this 'stunt'), Theodore and Llewelyn. Theodore's contribution was published separately as *The Soliloquy of a Hermit*, leaving only John and Llewelyn in the *Confessions*.

The book will disappoint anyone expecting revelations of the more sensational kind, for while the brothers dig deeply into their souls they provide no satisfaction for the prurient. John begins, surprisingly, with his intense awareness of his own hands, usually clumsy, helpless things which during his lectures become abnormally sensitive. 'I *feel* them as I speak; and between them and the waves of my thought there is a direct magnetic connection.' He remarks on the way his 'Roman Despot' appearance conceals a timidity 'natural rather to a slave than a master' and confesses (the word is appropriate at times) to being 'a tremendous and unconquerable egoist.' While devoid of a religious sense, he is thrilled with the idea of Jesus and wonders if there is something atavistic in this, 'a reversion in me to the medieval emotions of my ancestors'.

It is important to emphasise that Powys did not regard himself as a mystic, since some see him in this light. 'I know no human being less of a mystic than I am,' he says bluntly in *Confessions*, a point of view he never retracted. Again, he rejected pantheism.

> The idea of worshipping God in Nature, or worshipping Nature as God, has never had the remotest appeal for me. My instincts are all Polytheistic. A quite unmystical and perfectly naive worship of the sun or the moon or of any particular planet, is the sort of thing that I understand and sympathise with.
>
> (COTB, 61)

It is true that in time John Cowper Powys devised strange rituals involving the touching and embracing of trees and stones which held symbolic significance for him, but these should be seen as a highly personal means of obtaining practical help in coping with the pressures of existence rather than as a way of gaining insight into spiritual truths of universal application.

The *Confessions* reveals Powys to be a fatalist, believing the Universe to be determined by inexorable laws and his own life to be governed by the presence 'of a steady invincible mechanic force, pushing me forward from point to point, from stage to stage, and giving me no loophole of escape.' Fate 'sweeps us all forward, and the wisest and least wise among us are lucky if they can adjust themselves to its adamantine decrees, without the aching of their flesh and the envenoming of their heart's blood.' It is a tract undoubtedly influenced by the horror of war, but in which Powys explores a philosophy of resignation upon which he would expand in his latest works. Not least, he believes in the importance of self-acceptance.

> The margin of possible re-adaptation in everybody's life is necessarily small .... The important thing, it seems to me, is to recognise fully as quickly as possible both the limitations of one's own disposition and the limitations of one's circumstances, and to lose no time in adjusting one's self-assertion to these moulds.
>
> (COTB, 100)

It was an attitude which brought comfort to a man who was as painfully conscious of his inadequacies as ever. In a letter to Lulu (Llewelyn) from St Louis in November 1919, he saw himself as weak and cowardly, 'nothing but a wandering imagination'. His old vexation with his supposed failure as a writer nagged him remorselessly: 'Isn't it odd — here I am aged 47 and I haven't found my role in writing. All tour de forces! [sic] I am too light — an owl's feather, a night-jar's feather.'

For all that, another tour de force was taking shape: the most ambitious yet. *The Complex Vision,* first published in 1920, is the work of no lightweight but of an imaginative thinker who suggests that everything in creation is part of a living body embracing both animate and supposedly inanimate matter. For him, the contrast between living things and inert objects is a false one because all form part of the earth-body of our planet, which is itself subsumed into a cosmic over-soul. Individual consciousness is the key to the mystery: 'there is nothing in the world except personality'. The whole universe with all the bodies in it, including our own, is nothing but a manifestation of a single mind which is our own 'I am I'.

In this long, difficult and repetitious book Powys projects the idea of universes within universes making up a total reality which he came to think of as the Multiverse. There is much in *The Complex Vision* that anticipates themes in his novels, such as the concept of multiple realities co-existing with one another and his belief that consciousness of a kind exists not only in animal and vegetable life but in 'dead' matter also. Its abstruse and often clumsy language, however, in short the very complexity of *The Complex Vision*, makes it an unappealing work unlikely to open doors of understanding for many.

The book was written at a time when financial worries pressed heavily upon John Cowper Powys. Letter after letter to Llewelyn shows him to be in a depressed frame of mind in 1919-20. There were not enough lectures to provide him with the income he needed, his support for his wife being like a continual hole in the pocket. He even resorted to begging loans from his brother Littleton 'to keep Margaret going a bit,' but for all his worries he was determined to raise enough cash to send his son Littleton Alfred to Cambridge. There were no complaints about Arnold Shaw, who was still in charge of his lecturing itinerary. 'You know how nice he is and how linked together in this business he and I are,' Powys observed in a letter to Lulu, 'but the weight of his debts presses him down and at present with practically no lecturer but myself on his list it is hard for him to pick up'. Powys was desperate enough to try his hand at short stories, a literary form he despised. Plagued by money worries, beset by a sense of failure as a writer, he cast envious eyes in the direction of his father, now living in Weymouth with John's sister Gertrude. In a letter written from Missouri in January 1920, he exclaimed: 'How happy, though, to be like Father! nothing to do but walk and sleep and read the paper and look forward to one meal after another. No desires to harass him, no anxieties to disturb him — for of course his money will last!'

It seems that at this time everything had gone sour on John Cowper Powys. In that same letter he remarks on the 'characterless melancholy' of the Missouri landscape.

> Can it be the same planet and can this moon be the moon I have seen from Chanctonbury Ring and Lufton and Laon?

> Bricks over here don't seem bricks, trees don't seem trees; mud is not mud but some kind of dreary chemistry and the automata who nod and talk and get in and out of cars ... seem hardly to have those skulls and cross-bones within them that used to belong to the human race. But all the same I shall be all right and well-pleased if my lecture prospects improve ...
> (LTHBL, vol 1, 269)

His personal life had become complicated by the shakiness of Frances Wilkinson's marriage. She had become so unhappy with Louis that she turned to her old flame John for emotional support, taking her four-year-old son Oliver with her to share his rented house in California for a while. The arrangement also had its practical side, for she had heart trouble as well as suspected tuberculosis and it was felt that the visit would do her good. Oliver Marlow Wilkinson, the first child of her marriage to Louis Wilkinson, retained vivid memories of his godfather John Cowper Powys at this period. He was struck by the sweet, sharp scent that emanated from him, which he later found to be his shaving soap, and the carved coins and jewels that hung from his heavy watch chain. 'He was like a mineral,' he said in a conversation with the present author. To this perceptive and imaginative child, Powys's heavy English clothes seemed like the bark of a tree.

> Much later I came to think of him as like the clever one of a family of trees who had successfully studied to be a man. If you examine his writing, the people are interesting but my God! his fish, his stones, the weeds, the very earth is infinitely better. He was like something out of the earth.

Something else Wilkinson remembered, more than seventy years later, was the tension at meal times, when his mother and godfather argued fiercely over practically everything. So fraught were the child's nerves that on one occasion he shouted 'Stop it! Stop talking!' and to his surprise, they did. When he tried it again, however, he was firmly put in his place.

To young Oliver and his mother, John Cowper Powys was 'Signore Jack'. The small boy was aware of his mother's perception of him as a kind of magician, and he intuitively felt that his godfather could identify with a child's mind far more deeply than most adults. Powys was tolerant to a degree of Oliver's childish excesses, yet

when children overstepped the mark he would have a quiet word with their parents to ensure that for their own good they were brought to heel.

In a material sense, the tide turned for John Cowper Powys. New lecturing opportunities opened up and after a successful trip to the Mid West he was able to send Margaret 'quite a large sum' on his return to New York. With his own funds much healthier, Shaw mounted a series of lectures in New York in the spring of 1920, and Powys wired Margaret instructions not to let the house in the summer 'as I do want to see something of my son and he does so enjoy his holidays in Burpham'. With the change in his fortunes, Powys's whole outlook was transformed. He took pleasure in the new businesslike atmosphere he found in Shaw's office: 'it might be the office of Dombey and Son. It breathes stability and security,' he wrote approvingly to Llewelyn. His renewed confidence in Shaw, however, proved short-lived, and an important part of him remained unfulfilled. For all his professed hostility to the feminine principle, he needed women in his life. His charisma and literary fame, powerful aphrodisiacs both, had inevitably proved attractive to a variety of young women who attached themselves to him from time to time in America. He refers to them casually in his letters to his brother: Genefride, who 'chucked' him for newer and younger amorists, Dorothy, 'who says she doesn't want to be a plaything', and an unusual girl of Spanish-Jewish blood who for a while greatly occupied him.

> Never, Lulu my darling, was there such a face; never such flitting evasive — more than moth-like or fern-like or sea-weed-like — delicacy of expression and colour. And how tiny and slight her figure is. The other day she undid her hair for me, in one of the mountain woods here, and let it hang down over the edge of a mountain stream. You've never seen anything so bewitchingly lovely.
> (LTHBL, vol 1, 205)

He professed not to resent the fact that she would not let him touch her or kiss her ('isn't there wisdom in that?') and was impatient when Lulu impishly referred to her as a 'new well-beloved,' retorting: 'God forbid! Well-beloveds to Hell. I don't trust any of them.'

Frances was in a different category. Now living with Louis in London, she had as powerful a hold on him as ever. 'I begin to see clearly as I get older — you have spoilt me for ever for all others,' he confessed in a letter from Rochester NY in March 1920. But for ever is a long time, and unknown to him one other was in the wings, waiting to make an appearance.

Nine

John Cowper Powys first met Phyllis Playter in March 1921, when lecturing in the Mid-West state of Missouri. She was a young woman of intellectual tastes, something of a bluestocking, with literary ambitions much slighter than his own. She wanted to be a novelist, but was daunted by what she considered her shortcomings and apparently failed to complete a single novel. The daughter of an unusually bookish businessman who had settled in the small town of Joplin, she had a secretarial job in Kansas City. Small in stature, she was cursed with a neurotic temperament which resulted in frequent fits of depression. There were times when she contemplated suicide, more than half seriously.

There was something about this slight, frail woman that immediately appealed to Powys. She was exactly the physical type for which his soul craved, with the slim limbs he could associate with the ideal women of his imagination, and the intellectual sparks that flew between them excited and entranced him. The difference in their ages (she was twenty-eight, he approaching fifty) may have been a further stimulus. By the autumn he was hopelessly in love with her, pouring out his heart in letter after letter often written on hotel notepaper as he went from one lecture to another.

> I don't know what you've done to me. Don't go by what anyone says about me — I am what I am to you — I have written love letters before but this is different — there is a real mystery in this — I would like to cry and cry and cry.
> (NLW Ms)

His letters begin without any formality or endearments — no 'Dear' or 'Dearest' still less 'Darling' — but they are written with the fervour of the enraptured. 'I have never seen anyone like you except in my imagination — I miss you — I miss you most damnably,' he confesses. 'Oh thank the Lord we have met ... Nothing can divide us now.' He is almost beatifically conscious of the very ordinariness of their passion. 'Phyllis and Jack have just gone and fallen in love at first sight like lots of other Phyllises and Jacks so much less sophisticated than we are — Jacks and Phyllises who have not got any Aubrey Beardsley fixtures on their walls! Well, there it is!'

In these early days of the romance that was to endure until his death forty years later, he is almost painfully conscious of her vulnerability and is fearful for her, and for himself. She is, for him, a 'strange unhappy thing' whose self-destructive streak might yet deny him the happiness he is sure he can find with her. He urges her to 'bury those tablets of yours somewhere, at least a mile away from your house,' because she no longer belonged only to herself 'and you haven't the right to take away a horizon from another poor devil.' Just as he saw Frances as a sea-cat, so he sees Phyllis as a mad March hare, his admiration of her 'hare-like eyes' being a recurring theme in his diaries and letters. Quite what she made of his first protestations of devotion is impossible to tell, for they might have proved disconcerting to a more conventional woman. There is frequent praise of her thinness: he urges her to 'hold me tight against your bones — all flesh is vanity and illusion but the skeleton is real and I love your skeleton better than the rounded limbs of the darlings of pleasure.' At last the sylphs who had tormented his imagination in Brighton had found human shape. In one of the earliest of his undated letters in 1921 he writes:

> You are different — you are not an ordinary human girl. God knows what kind of a person you are! You are a mythological thing, an Undine, a sprite, a wounded elf, and I cling to you. With you I have hardly any sensuality — And yet it isn't asceticism — I don't know what it is — I think you are very near to Nature — you know? — I think the moods of Nature go straight through you — you are a tree a plant — you are air and water and earth — I don't care whether you have a heart or soul or a mind ...
>
> (NLW Ms)

From the first, he is keen to explain the part that his brother Lulu plays in his life. 'Lulu is an awfully absorbing person & we are much more like lovers than brothers — our relation is very unusual — but he wouldn't be jealous of you,' he writes from St Louis: rather too optimistically, as it turned out. Lyrical praise is heaped on the beloved: 'Do you think I have forgotten your hair like fine sea-weed across your forehead and your hare's eyes looking wild and soft out of its queer filmy strands in all the rain ...' But there is room also for more mundane matters. 'I cannot find any place where I can get even a passable cup of tea,' he complains from the Hotel Severn, Indianapolis. 'Oh dear! Oh dear! how wretched one can be in Middle Western cities!'

It is impossible to tell how Phyllis responded to these missives, since John Cowper Powys did not treasure people's letters as they treasured his. Since she does not appear to have discouraged his approaches, however, it is fair to assume that they were lovers (if not in the fullest sense) by the end of 1921. They lived separately until 1923, and even when she began to share his home in Patchin Place, New York, she did so tentatively at first, constrained by the sexual mores of the time: in *The Brothers Powys*, Richard Perceval Graves notes their pleasure in having the bohemian poet e.e. cummings for a neighbour. They could rely on his discretion, 'for they still did not like it to be generally known that they were living together, and occasionally the unexpected arrival of an acquaintance would compel Phyllis to pretend that she was just leaving, after which she had to wander the streets for an hour or two until the coast was clear' (TBP, 195). One of the things that impressed the young Isobel Powys Marks, visiting her Uncle Jack in the mid-1920s, was the fact that in some ways New York was less technologically advanced than she had been led to believe: the lavatory was two floors down and shared by the occupants of several apartments.

Although the relationship between John Cowper Powys and Phyllis Playter was common knowledge in his innermost circle, it was concealed from Margaret Powys for many years. Morine Krissdottir reveals in one of her notes in *Petrushka and the Dancer*, her selection of entries from the diaries of John Cowper Powys, that his wife and son and some of his relatives did not know of the liaison until 1934, when Littleton Alfred allowed his father to alter his will so as to include Phyllis in it. By then both John's parents were dead, the Rev Charles Francis Powys's remains having joined those of his wife in the family grave in Montacute in August 1923.

It was not only Llewelyn who felt jealous of Phyllis at first: John's sister Marian also resented her place in his affections. This is understandable, given the closeness of the relationship between John and

Marian, whom he always called May. Fearful of being lumbered with the task of caring for her parents in their old age, she had emigrated to New York in 1913, working first as a typist before opening a fashionable lace shop in Washington Square. She was a strong-minded woman possessed of what John saw as 'granite-based will-power'. He made no secret of his affection for her: 'I love her well — as well as we can love girls we can't have,' he told Llewelyn in a letter written in 1914. But did he, in fact, 'have' her in a physical sense? Suspicions of an incestuous affair (or at least some sexual play) between brother and sister have remained unproven, although Marian's illegitimate son Peter Powys Grey appears to have been convinced for the first twenty years of his life that John Cowper Powys was his father. Set against this is the fact that at the time of Peter's conception in the autumn of 1921, John was away from New York, lecturing in California and the western states. By then, too, he was deeply in love with Phyllis Playter. The 'authorised' version is that Peter Powys Grey, who was born in July 1922, was the son of the New York lawyer Ernest Angell. The name Grey was suggested by John, who when asked by Marian for his advice coolly observed that her moral position was neither black nor white but grey.

It must be noted that Peter Powys Grey's perception of John Cowper Powys was radically different in some respects from that of others. While those who knew him in later life in Wales saw him as a benevolent if somewhat eccentric figure, Grey carried forever a mental picture of a man who could be positively demonic. This arose from an incident when Grey, still a month short of his eighth birthday, followed Powys on a morning walk in the countryside and spied him urinating. Powys reacted furiously, rounding on the boy and bearing him kicking and yelling into the house, to the consternation of Phyllis Playter and the boy's mother. Powys purged himself of his rage by going to a hickory tree, kissing its soul (as he put it in his diary entry for that day in June 1930) and crying out, 'O help me to forgive Peter! O help me to forgive Peter!'

There was a streak of violence in John Cowper Powys, generally much subdued, which occasioned such bursts of ungovernable rages. Sometimes they came unexpectedly; Raymond Garlick remembers him railing against the novelist Henry James when Llewelyn's widow Alyse Gregory mentioned his name. Powys flailed his long arms and actually foamed at the mouth as he cried, 'I hate Henry James!' In a conversation with the present author, however, Garlick wondered whether Powys was angry not so much with James on this occasion as with Gregory.

It is easier to understand Powys's passionate outburst against the priests who, in his opinion, revelled in the opportunity to provide spiritual comfort to his dying son Littleton Alfred Powys in 1952. By then a Roman Catholic priest himself, Littleton was for a while nursed by nuns. A young woman then living in Corwen, Catrin Puw Morgan (later Davies) saw John Cowper Powys with his arms outstretched saying, 'They love it, they love suffering. Come along to see this lovely man, come along to see him suffering. Oh he is in pain and because God loves him the suffering is proof of his love.' Worn out by this fierce denunciation, Powys collapsed into a chair and sat there like someone in a trance.

After being possessed in this way, John Cowper Powys invariably sought to rid himself of the evil that had overtaken him. He believed strongly in the power of thought, a constant theme in his novels. To imagine sadistic scenes was to create a quiver in the atmosphere that would harm receptive souls; to hate someone was to cause damage to that person. Thus he appealed to the souls of trees to help rid him of this curse; sometimes he sought redemption in the earth itself. Outraged by the way he was parodied by his friend Louis (Marlow) Wilkinson in *The Buffoon* (though the buffoon in this novel is the Wilkinson-figure, not Powys), he sat under a tree and 'earthed' his hatred by digging his fists into the ground. In time he came to call the book 'admirable,' and to be 'sure no one reading it would accuse him (Wilkinson) of malicious intent,' so the earthing appears to have been successful.

Phyllis Playter, who from the time of their first meeting in 1921 played a central part in his life, offered not merely encouragement but literary advice which he valued. She read all his novels as they were being written and he took her comments to heart. She implored him not to cut *A Glastonbury Romance* when his publisher was asking him to do so, suggested making Magnus Muir in *Weymouth Sands* more like Powys himself, and was cross with him for 'wasting' his time on his philosophical books, even though these provided valuable additions to their income. 'She feels I ought to be a Novelist alone,' he writes in his diary in May 1932. Almost a decade earlier she had played an important part in persuading Powys to break finally with Arnold Shaw, whose performance as lecture manager had proved increasingly unsatisfactory; he had transferred first to Jessica

Colbert and then to the Lee Keedick Agency.

Playter was, in fact, not only lover (however we may interpret this) and companion, but critic and devoted upholder of his status as novelist. He, for his part, saw her as the mental, spiritual and physical embodiment of his feminine ideal; when they fell out he took all the blame upon himself. His diaries, semi-public in that he obviously intended them for publication and occasionally addressed his unknown readers in them, have frequent examples of his abasement before his beloved TT (which is generally acknowledged to mean Tiny Thin). There was, no doubt, something erotically satisfying in this; self-abasement has obvious sexual connotations, especially in one who admits to being a prey to sadistic impulses. But there is no denying the strength of the bond between John Cowper Powys and Phyllis Playter, nor the importance of this relationship in providing him with the inner security he required to write his greatest work.

As the 1920s advanced, John Cowper Powys appeared destined to spend the rest of his life in America. With his marriage to Margaret a mockery, existing in name only, there seemed no good reason why he should ever return permanently to England, still less make a home in Wales, the land of his very remote fathers. He had found an intellectual and social freedom in America which had been denied him in the class-ridden England of Victorian and Edwardian times, and he responded warmly to what he called 'certain free and noble aspects of life' in the New World. He was struck by the more relaxed relationship between the sexes and was captivated by American women, who made themselves exactly what they wanted to be.

> All American girls are potential actresses. They can 'make themselves up' for any mortal role on earth, from that of a Grand Duchess to that of a strolling gipsy. They actually decide upon what kind of accent and intonation they fancy will suit them best; and having decided on one that matches, let us say, their eyes and their hair, or the droop of their head, or the slenderness of their waist, or the warm depth of their bosom, they just *invent it* and then practice it till they are perfect in it. And this really is what they do with their whole character, their tastes, their tricks of manner, their ways of behaviour. All American women are, in fact, *made and not born*.
> (*Autobiography*, 514)

It is true that there were times when he hated America, railing against 'these unspeakable people and hideous streets and dreadful hotels,' but such disenchantment was generally induced by sheer weariness. 'But oh my friend and old companion, how I hate America and all this lecturing!' he cried in a letter to his brother Llewelyn in 1917. 'Am I destined to go on with this forever? Is there no escape?' He conjured up a picture of a demon beside him 'wagging his legs, in spats, to the tune of some vulgar American dance. They all jerk and jab and chatter and shove themselves about like galvanised puppets. They are not human.' More typical of his feelings for America are the essays he wrote for a variety of journals, mainly in the 1920s. They were brought together by Paul Roberts in *Elusive America*, Roberts noting in his introduction that America 'liberated Powys's creativity'. The essays, hitherto uncollected, display in abundance his affection for what he called 'the chaotic rough and tumble' of the American scene. He is susceptible to the infinite variety of the scenery and its effect on human character.

> I repeat once more — the essential spirit of America, its real contribution to civilization, is a psychic quality intimately associated with the geography of the continent, and far more involved with mystic nuances of feeling than the making of Arrow Collars, Chevrolets, caskets, plough-shares, chewing-gum, kodaks, dynamite and steel-rails .... For between this landscape and this character there has grown up a psychic reciprocity older than any science. What those old Indians breathed in from the earth-spirits of this land — an evasive sensitiveness in womankind, a rooted withdrawnness in mankind — can still supply its fluidity and its reserve to the modern mind that waits upon its spirit.
> (EA, 43)

Powys writes vividly about the pursuit of money in this society, but draws interesting conclusions. He saw it not as a vulgar get-rich-quick hunger for social prestige and possessions but as something laudable in itself. It was the pursuit of an ideal, 'the Platonic idea of power — power for its own sake ...' He notes the restlessness of Americans, their quizzical humour, and says that too much should not be read into their superficial braggadocio, which was but skin-deep. 'In one generation from his incoming a strange new reserve establishes itself in the nature of an immigrant; a reserve that underlies all his *brio* and all his effusive slang .... If American *culture* has a vaporous fluidity which it derives from its emancipated womanhood, American *character* has a rooted withdrawnness which it derives from its overworked manhood' (EA, 50).

Given his strong distaste for so many aspects of mass entertainment, it is difficult to drum up a vision of John Cowper Powys in Hollywood, that quintessential creation of the twentieth century. He went there early in the 1920s, however, when Charlie Chaplin was directing the film entitled *The Pilgrim*. Chaplin made such a favourable impression on Powys that he rated him one of the three greatest men he had ever met in his life, the others being Augustus John and Thomas Hardy. Much later he told Louis Wilkinson in a letter that what he learnt from 'Charlie C.' was to have 'some ideal of life for myself independent of everybody else'.

Powys was capable of great enthusiasm for other contemporary writers, a trait not universally shared in the envy-ridden world of professional authorship. During his American period he was especially supportive of the work of Theodore Dreiser, whose jagged lumps of social realism were not to everyone's liking. Powys defended Dreiser's preoccupation with sex in *The Genius*, while observing that a book was not necessarily good simply because its author was brave enough to tackle a taboo subject. 'An artist has a right to introduce into his work what he pleases and to exclude from his work what he pleases. The question for the critic is, not what subject has he selected, but how he has treated that subject: has he made out of it an imaginative, suggestive, and convincing work of art, or has he not!' (EA, 80).

Having got this off his chest, Powys proceeded to call *The Genius* 'an epic work,' and to find Dreiser concerned 'with the mass and weight of the stupendous life-tide; the life-tide as it flows forward, through vast panoramic stretches of cosmic scenery.' Powys was prepared to put his name to a letter of protest by novelists, dramatists, poets and others (including judges, doctors and clergy) against an attempt to suppress the book. In the event, the letter does not appear to have been published anywhere, but that in no way detracts from Powys's courage in standing out against this act of 'moral censorship.'

Powys also admired the work of the poet Edgar Lee Masters, author of *Spoon River Anthology*, which he called a 'great poem, the most original single volume of modern poetry that it has ever been my luck to find.' He thought that it had appeared (in 1915) at the right moment, 'when the literary youth of America was torn and divided between its irritation with the traditional academic school — the school of old men cringing before Europe — and its uneasy and dubious attraction to the appeals of new strange methods, methods that seemed to have no root and very little sincerity.' He went on:

> *Spoon River*, recognised at once as a work of unassailable and enduring value, set a new standard; a standard that demanded, in the first place, deep and authentic sincerity, and in the second place that indescribable quality, so hard to analyse, that we call 'style'. For this book has a style, as definite, as personal, as magical and arresting, as the style of Hawthorne or Poe or Whitman, or as Henry James himself. And yet it is a style, so fused and welded, so merged and lost, in the subject matter, that the subject matter seems, as we read, to be, so to say, *writing its own story*. This is nothing less than great art; when the impersonal and the universal are reached by means of the personal and the subjective.
> (EA, 106)

By the mid-1920s, John Cowper Powys was developing his own chosen art of novel-writing in significant ways. The decade saw the appearance of two of his novels and the inexplicable setting aside of a third which would not see light of day for another sixty years.

Part Two:
Life-Fulfilment

Ten

Once a novel was completed, Powys was congenitally incapable of picking it up and reading it again. Neither was he interested in taking up a work he had set aside, nor one which had suffered the indignity of rejection. Such inhibitions ensured that his third novel, *After My Fashion*, and his critical work on John Keats remained in limbo until long after his death.

There were, perhaps, other explanations for his suppression of *After My Fashion*, which he wrote in 1919. In his comprehensive work *The Brothers Powys*, Richard Perceval Graves notes that this novel relates closely to John's private life, dealing as it does with the problems of loyalty and deception in a modern marriage. In Graves's view, this 'may well be the reason why he made few, if any efforts to publish it during his lifetime.' The book did not find its way into print until 1980, when it was published with a foreword by Francis Powys, Theodore's son. In this, he notes that after bringing out *Wood and Stone* and *Rodmoor*, which sold poorly in spite of encouraging reviews, John Cowper Powys was contemplating writing a novel which would have Sussex for a background, 'with nature obtruding itself less, a quieter novel ...' He also notes that it was about this time that Powys met Isadora Duncan, an American dancer who was receiving high critical acclaim as a pioneer of free movement in dance. Her performances in New York, Paris and London were attended by all the avant-garde, and even in the wartime year of 1917 she was dashing enough to have plans to 'dance herself around the world through Japan and China'.

In the life of John Cowper Powys, Isadora Duncan was far more than a mere fellow-artist he simply happened to encounter. She was attracted to him originally through reading his *Visions and Revisions*, her enthusiasm being such that she sent him enough red roses to fill his flat in Greenwich Village. He confessed to Llewelyn that he was 'then too nervous to go and see her,' but once his nerves were overcome a friendship developed between them. 'We harmonised at once,' he declared, 'and of this I am really and legitimately proud, for in her own style she is as fine a genius as Nazimova or Sarah or Eleanora Duse.'

> She has been one of the most thrilling sensations — but that is a wretched word to express it — of my whole existence. She has danced for me alone — with a beauty that makes the most beautiful young girl's dancing seem mere child's play. It was as though Demeter herself, the mater dolorosa of the ancient earth, rose and danced.
> (LTHBL, vol 1, 242)

He assured Llewelyn that he was not in love with her, but that 'it has been one of the chief felicities of my life to have known her.' Her feelings for him were more volatile, for in January 1917 she sent him a lengthy telegram from California saying his soul had danced with hers and invitingly adding: 'Remember I am waiting for you here do not disappoint me I send you infinite love.' Somewhat boorishly, he called these 'salutations of an eccentric character' in a letter to Llewelyn shortly afterwards. She had, however, the consolation of a poem written in praise of her in *Mandragora*. More importantly, she inspired one of the most important characters in *After My Fashion*, the dancer Elise Angel, and probably also a subsidiary character in *A Glastonbury Romance*, Lisette. Interestingly, in both novels the male character concerned, Richard Storm in *After My Fashion* and John Crow in *A Glastonbury Romance*, feels guilty about 'fleeing' from the woman left behind in Paris. The intense relationship between Richard and Elise, which destroys his marriage, probably owes a great deal also to Powys's platonic love affair with Frances Gregg.

After My Fashion has an immediacy lacking in Powys's earlier novels, taking us into an England profoundly altered by the carnage of the trenches. The change is not so much external as in the psychology of young men such as Richard Storm, who returns home after unexceptional war service haunted by the sacrifices of the dead. Stretched out on the grass, enjoying the spring day, he broods on the way this much-loved landscape has been spared by 'the souls of the maimed and blighted, who had thrown their breathing, vibrating, passionate youthful bodies between the cruel engines of the invader and this fair country.'

Storm is a figure who shares both the appearance and the characteristics of his creator, not least his sense of family. His parents are dead, and he is on a pilgrimage to his grandparents' grave in the Sussex village of Littlegate. There he meets Nell, the vicar's daughter, and the strange Robert Canyot, a painter whom she intends to marry. Storm's guilt at surviving the war intact is intensified by the knowledge that Canyot is something of a war hero who lost his right arm in the fighting. Undaunted, he paints left-handed.

Storm's initial reaction to Nell is uncharitable, for he thinks her 'devilishly self-conscious' and 'a little prig,' lumping her also with the mass of womankind who 'can only be natural when they are fussing over you or being fussed over.' If this has much in it of Powys's attitude to his wife Margaret, as some critics have assumed, it tells us why the author was reluctant to see the book published.

Nell is torn between two men, Storm and Canyot, and Storm between two women, Nell and Elise. He marries Nell, but their decision to accompany Canyot to America turns out to be disastrous. Elise is appearing in New York and Storm renews his love affair with her. Nell, consumed by jealousy and expecting a child, turns to Canyot for emotional comfort. For Storm, the harsh cityscape of New York reflects his inner desolation.

> And what had he got now? Nelly's body was dominated by Nelly's child; Nelly's mind was dominated by Canyot. He had nothing for himself but odious duties and harassing responsibilities .... There were no fields or lanes in Manhattan where he could recover his spirit by drawing upon the deep earth forces. All about him were iron girders and iron cog wheels and iron spikes. All about him were the iron foreheads of such as partook of the nature of the machinery whose slaves they were. And the iron that entered his soul found no force that could resist it; for all the days of his life he had been an epicurean: when the hour called for stoicism he could only answer with a dogged despair.
>
> (AMF, 177)

Nell's disillusionment with Storm, and his reaction to it, are bleakly described and, as in *Rodmoor*, the book ends with the death of the hero.

Ducdame, Powys's third published novel, came out in 1925 in both New York and London. Its dedication to 'that superior man Kwang-Tse of Khi-Yuan' is almost certainly due to the influence of Phyllis Playter, who was a Taoist. The dedicatory note tells us that Kwang-Tse was 'the only one among philosophers to be at once respectful to his spirit-like ancestors and indulgent to those who, like the protagonist of this book, go where they are pushed, follow where they are led, like a whirring wind, like a feather tossed about, like a revolving grindstone.' All this gives a clue to the novel's themes. So does the Shakespearian title, which recalls Jaques's explanation in *As You Like It* that the word 'ducdame' is 'a Greek invocation, to call fools into a circle'.

The protagonist, Rook Ashover, is another John Cowper Powys-like figure. He is living with his mistress, Netta Page, but has several women vying for his attention: Netta herself, his cousin Ann, the vicar's wife Nell and, not least, his mother. What troubles his mother most is that Netta, whom she dislikes anyway, is incapable of bearing Rook a child, which means that the long line of Ashovers of Ashover Hall will come to an end with Rook. There is a strong bond between Rook and his sickly brother Lexie which, as in *Wood and Stone*, gives a fictional slant to the John-Llewelyn relationship. Rook's ability to attract women puzzles Lexie: 'What do you do to all these women, Rook, to make them so fond of you?' he asks. The truth is that Rook does very little; it is as much a puzzle to him as to anyone.

A sense of family is far more dominant and menacing in *Ducdame* than in *After My Fashion*. The Ashover dead are a continual presence, silently urging Rook to produce a son and heir so that the family line might endure. They haunt him even when kissing Nell (recklessly, in the church where the dead lay buried).

> He was aware of an angry menace rising from all that human dust under his feet, threatening him if he did not open the gates of the future to their race, cursing him if he barred and locked those gates in the selfish enjoyment of uncreative, unproductive emotion.
>
> As he caressed her there in that dark church on that curious day he felt as though he were inflicting a definite wound upon the accumulated yearning, the gathered tension, stretching out into the future, of six long human centuries.
>
> So many fathers begetting so many children; so many children begetting so many fathers; and all to end in his striking them back into the annihilating dark, with a mocking 'Down, wantons, down!'
>
> (*Ducdame*, 85)

The wantons, however, triumph. Cousin Ann's subtle campaign to win Rook succeeds when she traps him into sleeping with her, and her pregnancy ensures that they marry. In a conclusion that echoes the melodrama of *Rodmoor*, Rook is murdered by Nell's husband, the mad priest William Hastings, just when Ann is giving birth to their son.

For all its weaknesses this is in many respects a powerful novel in which the author confidently handles the complexity of Rook's personal relationships. The increasing maturity of his writing shows itself, too, in the way the Dorset landscape is not merely described but influences the lives of his characters. Memorably, the dead leaves on a still December day give forth a savour 'of the very sweat of death itself,' acting on the nerves of women because it 'answers to one of their own most profound and secret moods'. Rook, however, hates such a day.

> He felt a queer, nervous, reluctant uneasiness even about meeting Nell. He would have given anything for a hard, nipping black frost to get a grip upon these misty meadows, to turn all this clinging earth-flesh into frozen rock! He loathed the sodden, relaxed clay with its incense-reek of insidious mortality. He longed to escape from it all, into some clear, purged, bitter air. He felt homesick for the tang of the salt, unharvested, unfecund sea.
> (*Ducdame*, 80)

Ducdame marks the end of a phase in Powys's life, both as man and artist. It is the last of his 'prentice novels, which in their themes and obsessions presage the mature work which won him his reputation. But it is surely no coincidence that from now on he has the steadying influence of Phyllis Playter in his life, providing not only domestic comfort but psychological support. The death-obsession which has led Powys to construct such violent (and, it must be said, banal) fates for his heroes gives way to a broader canvas and firmer grasp of fictional possibilities. The stage is set for the true artist to lay the ghost of Moony, strutting his manic dance on the verge of a blackness which he fears might wholly consume him.

Powys had already begun writing the first of his major novels, *Wolf Solent*, at the time of *Ducdame's* publication, but it was not to appear in print until 1929. The years between had seen him continuing the lecture tours which, however exhausting, provided him with his main income and an overall view of America such as few obtain. From train windows he observed 'the shack-littered banks of the Mississippi or the "Blood of Christ" mountains of New Mexico, or the Osage hedges of Kansas, or the huge red barns with their stately silo-towers of Wisconsin.' Back home in New York's Greenwich Village, he enjoyed walks with Phyllis Playter along Wall Street to the East River docks, peering along the way into 'dark cavernous oily ship-chandlers' shops piled with rope and coal-shovels and lanterns'. Their apartment in Patchin Place had a 'marvellously sequestered atmosphere' for the writer, Fred Blair, who visited them in August 1928. He found 'an air of artistically arranged rusticity' there, 'the conscious expression, no doubt, of a man buried in Manhattan with his memories of the English countryside.' He was invited to sit down in a wicker-work chair that had a large hole in the middle of the seat, its venerable appearance persuading him to wonder, rather fancifully, if the Powys ancestor William Cowper had sat in it while writing 'The Task'.

Blair, a young man with a sharp eye and decided opinions, found more than a hint of the archetypal American Pioneer Woman in Phyllis Playter, whose 'sober dignity' and 'demurely chiselled physiognomy' made an impression on him. Powys was 'older and much more rugged and weathered' than he had imagined, and his quiet conversation made a striking contrast with his grand manner on the platform. The only things suggestive of his public speaking, in fact, were 'the subtle, subdued gestures of his voice and hands'.

Blair notes that at this time Powys was enjoying a reputation as 'the most elegantly-exotic creature known to American lecture addicts,' with a great following among women. They would, no doubt, have found him an even more fascinating and dangerous figure than they imagined had they known things about him which were concealed from the general public. There was his interest in the occult, fostered by Louis Wilkinson, which led to a strange experience during Wilkinson's honeymoon voyage to England with his bride Frances Gregg in 1912, when they were accompanied by John Cowper Powys and his sister Marian. A letter from 'Jack' to Frances's mother recounts how on 16 April, two days after the sinking of the Titanic, they drew the red curtains around them and tried table turning. 'A spirit from the drowned Titanic was there, called "Laroche". He said, "Frightful Disaster, assumed name, foreign affairs, my love, madness, madness ..."' Louis's son Oliver Marlow Wilkinson has noted how, when the party checked a casualty list, they actually found the name 'Laroche' on it. 'The event was well authenticated and the "message" was reported to the Society for Psychical Research,' he writes.

Powys's letters to Llewelyn reveal that he had 'strange presentiments' at the beginning of the fateful year of 1914, when he was in Boston with Louis, Frances and her mother. 'I don't at all like the look of 1914,' he remarked, in a letter which described how they were telling fortunes with cards. 'My fortune for 1914 has always been sinister — hers (Frances's) also — Louis's better, but the Ace of Spades the Death Card, continually turning up with him.'

Powys came to know Aleister Crowley, a kind of devil's disciple who preached, among other things, a gospel of sexual liberation. He called himself 'the Great Beast' and grew accustomed to judicial censure, Mr Justice Swift once belabouring him for writing 'horrible, blasphemous and abominable stuff'. The press thought him capable of anything, dubbing him 'the wickedest man in the world'. Crowley, a self-proclaimed magician, numbered Louis Wilkinson among his followers. When Frances (Gregg) Wilkinson opposed their friendship Crowley tried to get her certified insane. This was too much for Powys, who spoke of 'that thrice-damned devil Aleister Crowley trying to throw his infernal spells over Frances, nearly scaring her to death.' Noting that Crowley had 'taken half of a fancy to *Rodmoor*', Powys declared that this made him feel 'as if I had written one of those awful books such as I used once to buy — but never again, sweet Christ! — never again.'

The 'awful books' were the sadistic works for which he had once hungered, hiding them away with a sense of shame and self-disgust. Now he no longer needed them, yet there was much that was strange and inexplicable about him. He was apparently involved in at least two out-of-body experiences, one in America and the other in Wales. On the first occasion, according to Oliver Marlow Wilkinson:

> He told Theodore Dreiser he was making a journey the following day and Dreiser expressed regret that he wouldn't be seeing him. He said 'Dreiser, I will be with you at 2 o'clock tomorrow precisely.' At 2 o'clock next day Dreiser looked up and there was Jack, observed as clearly as if he had actually been there. Then the image slowly faded.

John Batten relates a similar story. It was told him by Peter Powys

Grey, a few weeks before his death in October 1992. Grey recalled how, shortly after his marriage, he took his bride to meet John Cowper Powys and Phyllis Playter in Corwen. Taking exception to Grey's light-hearted account of the wedding, especially his account of the eccentric behaviour of the officiating cleric, Powys burst out, 'How dare you make fun of a man of the cloth!' Grey, who had suffered from his uncle's temper as a child, hastily retreated with his bride to the hotel where they were staying at the foot of a steep hill immediately below Powys's home in Cae Coed. This was most easily approached, writes Batten, by a zig-zag road.

> There was, however, an alternative, direct but precipitous, path down the escarpment, fit only for the reckless and nimble of foot. It was this they took, slipping and sliding, hand-in-hand, coming to rest in the foyer of the hotel, breathless but filled with relief at their escape. At that moment, and before they had uttered a word, the swing-doors burst open, framing J.C.P., towering like a thunder-cloud, and shouting 'No tea! No tea!': and then they closed and he was gone.

The only detail Peter could recall afterwards, was that John was wearing boots which were unlaced. It was his absolute conviction that no man over seventy, even with his boots laced, could have taken that track down the hill, and he could not possibly have arrived that quickly by road. Years later, after John Cowper's death, Peter spent several days with Phyllis in London. For reasons he never understood, he did not ask her about the events of that day or the apparition at the hotel (PSN no 21, 21).

It is true, of course, that John Cowper Powys always thought of himself as a magician, and although the word can be interpreted in many ways there was something about him that persuaded people to suspend disbelief. For his godson Oliver Marlow Wilkinson, 'John Cowper Powys used magic of the mind. He manipulated will and emotion, psychologically in part, but reaching beyond the rational.' And, memorably, he summarised what are perhaps the most striking aspects of his genius.

> John Cowper Powys had talent in describing a person; genius in describing a fish: even more genius in describing the water in which the fish swims, and the stones on the floor of the stream. He himself was more plant than animal; more mineral

than either. He was dust and rock and feather and fin talking with a man's tongue.

He had some care for the technique of his arts, but, over all, he proclaimed that he had such a line on the Universe that he had no need for style. His writing, in its deepest intention, is incantation.

(SF, 15)

Eleven

Wolf Solent was, for John Cowper Powys, an imagined home-coming. The novel opens with its eponymous hero going back to his native Dorset by rail, filled with an excitement tinged with anxiety as to what the outcome of this epic journey might be. The fiction reflects the author's circumstances, for he began the book while travelling across America to and from lecturing engagements.

In 1960, thirty-one years after the novel first appeared, Powys wrote a preface for a new edition in which he called it 'a book of Nostalgia, written in a foreign country with the pen of a traveller and the ink-blood of his home.'

> As I wrote *Wolf Solent* travelling through all the states of the United States except two, I became more and more intensely aware of the hills and valleys, the trees and various flowers, the lanes and hedges and ponds and ditches, of the country round Sherborne; with the Abbey and the Preparatory School and the Big School; and also of the Great House and Lake, a mile or so away.
>
> (WoS, vii)

Fiction, however, is not autobiography, and such places were transfigured in his imagination into a landscape peculiar to this novel. It is one infused by Powys's imaginative response to nature. This shows itself not only in set-piece descriptions of the natural scene which are among the finest in English literature, but also in almost throwaway similes that might easily be missed. Thus newly-budded plane trees 'cast curious little shadows, like deformed butter-flies, upon the yellowish paving-stones,' and a steel-grey sky 'seems to hold within it a suppressed whiteness, like the whiteness of a sword that lies in shadow'. This feeling for the natural world is sometimes internalised in a way that throws light on the dominant character, Wolf Solent, who like his creator sees himself as being involved in a cosmic struggle between opposing powers.

> Wolf himself, if pressed to describe it, would have used some simple earthly metaphor. He would have said that his magnetic impulses resembled the expanding of great vegetable leaves over a still pool — leaves nourished by hushed noons, by liquid, transparent nights, by all the movements of the elements — but making some inexplicable difference, merely by their spontaneous expansion, to the great hidden struggle always going on in Nature between the good and evil forces. (WoS, 8)

At the heart of the novel lies Wolf's life-illusion, his sense of his own identity which is threatened by the events that take place after his return to the county he had left as a child of ten. Again like Powys, Wolf employs a psychological safety device which he calls his 'mythology,' a means of gathering together his inner forces in defence of his own integrity as a human being. We are told that he uses the word 'entirely in a private sense of his own,' dating back to the time when, as a child sitting in the bow-window of his grandmother's house in Weymouth, he deliberately explored the depths of his being.

> This 'sinking into his soul' — this sensation which he called 'mythology' — consisted of a certain summoning-up, to the surface of his mind, of a subconscious magnetic power which from those very early days, as he watched the glitter of sun and moon upon the waters from that bow-window, had seemed prepared to answer such a summons.
>
> This secret practice was always accompanied by an arrogant mental idea — the idea, namely, that he was taking part in some occult cosmic struggle — some struggle between what he liked to think of as 'good' and what he liked to think of as 'evil' in those remote depths.
>
> How it came about that the mere indulgence in a sensation that was as thrilling as a secret vice should have the power of rousing so bold an arrogance, Wolf himself was never able to explain; for his 'mythology,' as he called it, had no outlet in any sort of action. It was limited entirely to a secret sensation in his own mind, such as he would have been hard put to it to explain in intelligible words to any living person.
>
> But such as it was, his profoundest personal pride — what

> might be called his dominant *life-illusion* — depended entirely upon it.
> (WoS, 8)

All the events in the novel are seen from the standpoint of Wolf Solent, a man in his mid-thirties who has given up teaching to write a peculiar history of Dorset for the local squire, Urquhart; peculiar in that it is to concentrate on scandals and crimes, 'the sort of perspective on human occurrences that the bedposts in brothels must come to possess,' as Urquhart puts it. Wolf sees Urquhart as the embodiment of evil, and it is his submission to him, especially in his acceptance of money for writing a book he despises, which plays a crucial part in destroying his life-illusion. As a character, however, Urquhart is far less central to the book's narrative than the two young women who are rivals for Wolf's affections: Gerda, the child of nature whom he marries, and the more intellectual and complex Christie. Once again we are in the hothouse of sexual jealousy as Wolf, torn apart by conflicting loyalties like Richard in *After My Fashion* and Rook in *Ducdame*, is forced to accept that Christie's intrusion into his sensibilities has destroyed his happiness with Gerda.

> Why had he married her at all? That was the whole blunder! He had married her because he had seduced her. But girls were always being seduced! *That* was no reason. No! He couldn't get out of it. He had married her because he had mistaken a mixture of lust and romance for love; and if he hadn't found Christie, he might, to the end of his days, never have discovered his mistake! Affection would have superseded lust; tenderness would have superseded romance. All would have been well. It was Christie's appearance that had changed everything; and there it was!
> (WoS, 251)

Overcoming a death wish, Wolf finally comes to terms with his fate, reflecting that every soul is alone and that one must either endure or escape.

Wolf Solent, the first of the four Wessex novels which established John Cowper Powys's reputation, is probably the best introduction to his work for the reader unfamiliar with his novels. Its memorable characters include Selena Gaunt, a woman of preposterous ugliness who once had an ambiguous relationship with Wolf's father, the sinister bookseller Malakite and the poet Jason Otter, who combines childish mischievousness with a thinly disguised malice. There are robust descriptions of the kind of social events which do not figure in his early novels, such as horse fairs and village fêtes, and inspired passages in which a cloudy sky can become a passport to a magical land.

> Though the sky was overcast, it was overcast with such a heavenly 'congregation of vapours' that Wolf would not have had it otherwise. There were filmy clouds floating there that seemed to be drifting like the scattered feathers of enormous albatrosses in a pearl-white sea; and behind these feathery travellers was the milky ocean on which they floated. But even that was not all; for the very ocean seemed broken here and there into hollow spaces, ethereal gulfs in the fleecy whiteness; and through these gulfs was visible a pale yellowish mist, as if the universal air were reflecting millions of primrose buds! Nor was even this vaporous luminosity the final revelation of those veiled heavens. Like the entrance to some great highway of the ether, whose air-spun pavement was not the colour of dust, but the colour of turquoise, there, at one single point above the horizon, the vast blue sky showed through. Transcending both the filmy whiteness and the vaporous yellowness, hovering there above the marshes of Sedgemoor, this celestial Toll-Pike of the Infinite seemed to Wolf, as he walked towards it, like some entrance into an unknown dimension, into which it was not impossible to pass! Though in reality it was the background of all the clouds that surrounded it, it seemed in some mysterious way nearer than they were. It seemed like a harbour into which the very waters of the Lunt might flow. That incredible patch of blue seemed something into which he could plunge his hands and draw them forth again, filled like overflowing cups with the very ichor of happiness. Ah! That was the word. It was *pure happiness*, that blue patch!
>
> (WoS, 138)

In 1930, the year following *Wolf Solent's* publication in both New York and London, Powys brought out *In Defence of Sensuality*, probably the most stimulating and most readable of his philosophical books. It is unashamedly hedonistic in tone, arguing that 'every kind of sex-sensation is good' and that the secret of life is simply to enjoy it 'in a certain way, and with a certain quality of enjoyment'. What he has in mind is not a passive kind of pleasure but a happiness deliberately sought, with all the force of the will behind it. The art of forgetting unpleasant memories or present circumstances is an essential part of the process, for this willed happiness is summoned up from the depths of one's being: the sense of 'I am I' which is the bedrock of one's consciousness. Powys calls this the 'ichthyosaurus-ego' because it emphasises 'the remote vegetable-reptile-saurian background of the human soul.'

In the Powys philosophy, the remote past and the remote future are to be found in equal measure. The kind of goodness found in a saint comes from the future, is in fact 'a mysterious "entelecheia" or premonitory rumour of a non-human, godlike state of being, in which humanity will be merged, lost, surpassed.' By then men and women will have become as gods, reaching a stage of evolution in which they will have changed into 'something different from humanity'.

Powys was always aware of his privileged position as one born into the bourgeoisie, and it is easy to deride such a philosophy of life as one much simpler to hold in a state of material comfort than in poverty. Yet his argument that it is possible to squeeze happiness from elements in even the most dire personal circumstances is a persuasive one. He is fond of conjuring up the image of yellow sunlight falling on a wall, wherever that wall might be, and the simple pleasure it is possible to take in contemplating it, even though one might be in a sick-bed. He speaks of the 'simple primeval happiness in the immediate experience of being alive,' watching the clouds pile up, catching the silhouettes of bare branches against a November sky, sitting over a fire 'thinking the long thoughts of vague race-memories — all these things, belonging to a world of psychic-physical sensations that go back to the beginnings of consciousness, are the stuff of which the secret of life is made.'

Passionately, he argues the need of 'a John the Baptist of the senses' to baptise us 'into the ecstasy of simply being alive upon the earth' and, more quietly, he insists that the kind of calm, unruffled contemplation which he advocates as the purpose of life can be practised in every situation.

> A railway-porter can practise it. An engineer can practise it. A miner can practise it. A farm-labourer can practise it. A soldier or a sailor can practise it. A factory-worker or a

1. John Cowper Powys (extreme left) with his brothers Littleton, Theodore, Albert (Bertie), Llewelyn and William, outside Montacute Vicarage.

2. Frances Gregg (right), who married Louis (Marlow) Wilkinson, with her mother, Julia Vanness Gregg and grandmother, Gertrude Heartt.

3. Phyllis Playter wearing Breton costume while on a visit to France.

4. Portrait of John Cowper Powys in his early lecturing days in America.

5. John Cowper Powys with his sister Marian and dog, The Black, at Phudd Bottom, where John and Phyllis Playter lived for some years.

6. Two lifelong friends – John Cowper Powys (right) with Louis (Marlow) Wilkinson, outside 1 Waterloo, Blaenau Ffestiniog.

7. Louis (Marlow) Wilkinson with Llewelyn Powys.

8. John Cowper Powys with his son Littleton Alfred (a Roman Catholic priest) at Valle Crucis Abbey near Llangollen.

9. John Cowper Powys in his early 60s, relaxing – somewhat studiously – outside 7 Cae Coed, Corwen with his dog The Black.

10. The pair of houses in Manod, Blaenau Ffestiniog, named Waterloo. Powys and Playter lived in no 1, the Roberts family next door.

11. John Cowper Powys at 1 Waterloo.

12. John Cowper Powys with two Welsh people whose friendship he treasured – Benson Roberts (left) and the poet Huw Menai.

13. John Cowper Powys as many people remember him – writing his books on the couch in the upstairs room at 1 Waterloo.

> shop-assistant can practise it. Even a banker can practise it — although it is probable that the hired-man who works in his garden has a much better opportunity for such a deep, secret, magical-sensuous state of being than his master.
> (IDOS, 165)

By now a sea-change was taking place within John Cowper Powys. Weary with the rigours of the lecture circuit, he longed to renounce it and to devote all his energies to writing. A visit with Phyllis Playter to Hillsdale in Columbia County in September 1929, one hundred miles north of New York City, had a profound effect on him. He drew water from a well, lit the stove 'like Wolf', found a stream with alders growing beside it, and discovered an apple tree which reminded him of one they used to climb in the orchard at Montacute. What is more, literary soul that he was, he read Malory aloud to Phyllis and found it getting 'more and more exciting.' He returned to New York City in a dissatisfied mood, longing to move to Hillsdale but finding Phyllis unimpressed with the idea. Arguments with his lecture agent Lee Keedick did not help.

Later that year, he took part in a public debate with Bertrand Russell on the question, 'Is Modern Marriage a Failure?' Setting his own experience aside, he argued that it was not. The debate was held on 13 December 1929 in a public hall in New York, and such was the interest that two thousand people turned up. Russell argued that marriage was rooted in jealousy to such an extent that it was a 'restrictive and bad institution and the cause of unhappiness'. Powys, on the other hand, thought that it fulfilled 'the nobler nature, the subtler nature ... and the more rational nature of human beings'. Since he had been living happily with his mistress for several years and was seeing very little of his wife, he was either showing Olympian detachment or being deeply hypocritical. At the end of the debate, 1,010 of those present voted for Russell and 990 for Powys. A mock-up of the debate, filmed seven days earlier at the Fox movie studios in what Powys called 'an atmosphere of greenish malign grotesquerie and gross crudity', shows him making an imaginary speech and gesticulating 'like a mandarin'. He speaks in an oddly stilted way which much have contrasted sharply with his normal lecturing manner.

His usual summer visit to England in 1929 had found him visiting his wife, who was still unaware that he was living with Phyllis

Playter, and some of his brothers and sisters. He was already planning his next novel, to be set in Glastonbury, and resolved to work 'hard and steadily at the book' during a visit to the town in August.

In London, Powys called on the novelist Dorothy Richardson, whose work he admired, and his brother Bertie, the architect Albert Reginald Powys. These visits followed a tender meeting in Sussex with Frances Gregg, whom he found 'mellower, wiser, gentler, more tolerant of the weakness of her fellow-creatures'. He confided to her that his book *The Meaning of Culture* (which came out in New York in 1929 and in London the following year) was intended as 'a sort of hand-book of self-culture for the young boys and girls of my adopted land.' His background reading for the Glastonbury novel took him into the world of the Welsh scholar Sir John Rhys, whose book on the Arthurian Legend he found absorbing. In his diary, which he faithfully wrote up every day, he noted that he had now 'got on the track of the mythological Graal [sic] far older than the Holy Graal.'

Returning to New York, he resumed his lecture tours despite the continuing misery of stomach ulcers, but at last persuaded Phyllis of the need to move out of the city. 'O may she be happy there!' he cried, contemplating the move to Hillsdale. It came in April 1930, when they bought a timber-framed cottage which they called Phudd Bottom. In *Petrushka and the Dancer*, Morine Krissdottir relates how they set about improving a primitive house with the help of local handymen. For all the difficulties he was happy, not least because he was able to make a start on the novel that came to be called *A Glastonbury Romance*. 'May I be inspired by all the spirits of all hills; and of all stones upon all hill-sides and upon all plains raised up above sea-level,' he wrote in his diary, in prose reminiscent of the rolling cadences of the Church of England's Litany. Phyllis, however, was finding it hard to settle in a rural environment that must have contrasted painfully with the sophistication of Greenwich Village. 'The T.T. finds this world a *very* difficult place,' he observed in midsummer. 'She must have come from some quiet Cimmerian land where the sun always shines through mother of pearl.'

Unquestionably, however, the move to upstate New York was the right one for Powys. Free at last of the tyranny of the lecture circuit, he had the time to devote himself entirely to his writing, in the serene environment for which his soul had craved. The landscape reminded him of England, with its carefully planted hedges and picturesque stone walls.

> These walls give me, as an Englishman, a recurrent shock of surprise and pleasure. They are exactly like the stone walls of Derbyshire, my native county in England, but ... they have a look that, to my eyes, has something idealized about it — too mellow and too beautiful to be quite real — a look as if they belonged to some fabulous Arcadia where the walls had slowly subsided into the kindly earth by reason of there being no person nor animal against whom they assert exclusive property rights.
> (EA, 196)

He was captivated by 'the *roundness* of the wooded hills,' and was struck by their resemblance to the 'Mount Cloud' he had shaped out of the wet soil in the vicarage garden at Shirley in his childhood. Winter, with its deep snows, was a 'heavenly Nirvana' that freed him from 'the teasing bustle of Being'; but the most wonderful thing of all, for him, was the strange golden light that fell most often in the spring, 'a rich medieval red-gold light' that made those hills 'like enchanted forests in an ancient Teutonic fairy-tale.'

It was here that his Glastonbury story began to take shape, his characters to fill out in the magical process of creation. Some resembled the author; others were nothing like him whatsoever. In their richness and diversity they mark a major advance in his powers as a writer; and in his creation of a novel huge not only in size but also in ambition and complexity, he justified his claim to be a magician transforming reality for those brave enough to follow him.

Twelve

A *Glastonbury Romance* has probably given rise to more theorising than any other novel by John Cowper Powys. Its almost perversely plain title tells us that it can be accepted simply as the kind of long narrative which Powys, an ardent admirer of Walter Scott and Charles Dickens, enjoyed reading so much from his youth into old age. Its subject matter and allusions, however, the richness of its text and, above all, the sense it invokes in us of being in a world of the imagination in which few things can be taken at face value, invite the reader to look beneath the surface in search of more recondite meaning.

The legend of the Grail is central to the novel, but it is not necessarily the Christian Holy Grail that Powys has in mind. In his preface to the 1955 edition of the novel, published twenty-three years after its first appearance, he tells us that what he first found alluring about the Grail 'were the unholy elements in both its history and its mystery; in other words the unquestionable fact that it was much older than Christianity itself'.

> Christianity instinctively clutched at it as an ideal receptacle for the Blood of the Redeemer; but it has other levels of reception in its sacrosanct grillage, and it remains a dedicated symbolic centre for all those primordial cosmic 'fetishes' which are the broken, baffled, but ever-returning visions of some sort of conscious identity after death, visions that hint indeed at strange degrees of consciousness in a world which, though as material as you please, remains, with all its offspring, insubstantial as the stuff of dreams.
> (AGR, xiii)

Glastonbury had stirred his imagination from childhood, ever since his father pointed out its Tor to him from the slopes they had climbed from the vicarage at Montacute. Dimly visible in the distance across the broad West Country acres, it came to symbolise the magical view of life he held so dear. Wreathed in Arthurian legend, the repository of ancient cults, it was the perfect setting for a novel in which his most profound sense of the mysteries of existence would find expression. Its most arresting figure, the faith healer John Geard who becomes mayor of Glastonbury, embodies Powys's sense of the infinite power of humanity, if natural instincts and forces be given free rein, and his tragic death may perhaps encapsulate a Powysian belief that what the gods decree cannot be avoided.

This novel is not for the faint-hearted, nor those easily put off by extraordinary concepts uncompromisingly expressed. Its opening paragraph has probably lost far more potential readers than it has gained.

> At the striking of noon on a certain fifth of March, there occurred within a causal radius of Brandon railway station and yet beyond the deepest pools of emptiness between the uttermost stellar systems one of those infinitesimal ripples in the creative silence of the First Cause which always occur when an exceptional stir of heightened consciousness agitates any living organism in this astronomical universe. Something passed at that moment, a wave, a motion, a vibration, too tenuous to be called magnetic, too subliminal to be called spiritual, between the soul of a particular human being who was emerging from a third-class carriage of the twelve-nineteen train from London and the divine-diabolic soul of the First Cause of all life.
>
> (AGR, 21)

The breathtaking scope of this statement, the juxtaposition of stellar emptiness and the twelve-nineteen from London, and the sense of a Janus-faced First Cause involving itself with a single human organism, brings us up short. Clearly, this book will present us with no religious or philosophical orthodoxy; and are all those words really necessary? It is John Cowper Powys at his most challenging; he either holds us or repels us.

If we stay with him, however, he swiftly engages us in the destiny of John Crow, 'a frail, thin, loosely-built man of thirty-five' who has just abandoned a precarious life in Paris, leaving behind him (like Richard Storm) a young woman with whom he was emotionally involved. He encounters his cousin Mary and almost instantly begins a love affair with her, seeing her as 'an undine out of Harrod's Mill-pond'. They both attend the funeral of their grandfather Canon William Crow, who like Powys's own maternal grandfather lived in East Anglia. The reading of his will reveals that he has left practically everything to his former secretary-valet, John Geard, who has already quit the rectory to rejoin his family in Glastonbury. It is this bequest, so outrageous to John's materialistic cousin Philip Crow, that sets in train the events on which the novel turns.

Undismayed, John Crow sets off to walk to Glastonbury, where Mary is employed as companion to the elderly spinster Euphemia Drew. On the way he encounters Owen Evans, a Welshman who offers him a lift in his car. Evans incorporates aspects of John Cowper Powys in his personality; in particular an obsession with sadism of a cerebral kind. An antiquarian, he possesses books which satisfy his lust for images which he recognises as evil. One especially torments him: the image 'concerned with a killing blow delivered by an iron bar.' He believes that if he could see the Grail he would be cured; but, perversely, he does not want to see it.

Writing out of his own experience, Powys invests the suffering of Evans with horrible immediacy. The scenes of sadistic cruelty that dwell in the 'back chambers' of his mind make 'his pulses beat, his blood dance, his senses swoon, his knees knock together.'

> The taste of the least of these loathsome scenes was so overpowering to him that it reduced all the rest of life — eating, drinking, working, playing, walking, talking — to tedious occurrences, that had to be got through but that were wanting entirely in the electric quiver of real excitement. What Mr Evans suffered from was a fever of remorse such as cannot very often have taken possession of human minds in the long course of history. To say that the unhappy man wished that he had never been born would be to put the case mildly. Like Othello he longed to bathe in 'steep-down gulfs of liquid fire'.
> (AGR, 109)

Evans informs John Crow that Geard's wife Megan belongs to the ancient Welsh family of Rhys, and that he sees in the Geards' daughter Cordelia 'the very spirit of the old Cymric race'. Thus the building blocks of this long novel, more than 500,000 words in length, are steadily laid. It is a novel in which Arthurian and other

Welsh legends intertwine with myths relating to the Grail and tales of early Christianity. Yet there are other, bolder themes: the power and perils of sexual attraction, the conflict between capital and labour at a time when Communism was seen by many (not least those born into bourgeois comfort like John Cowper Powys) as the only way forward. Powys puts all such questions into a human framework by creating characters who live and breathe, and who act out their destinies in as chaotic a fashion as in the 'real' world that exists outside the pages of fiction. It is a loosely-structured novel in which dramatic opportunities are carelessly, almost wilfully, discarded. What might have been the climax of a lesser work, the Midsummer Pageant in Glastonbury during which Owen Evans nearly dies in simulating the suffering of Christ on the Cross, merely marks the end of the first of the novel's two volumes. Yet once we are impaled on Powys's hook, we are carried irresistibly forward. The final chapter finds Geard (Bloody Johnny, who has miraculously cured a woman of breast cancer) drowning in a flood, seeing a vision of the Grail at the last. Flawed the novel may be; self-indulgent it undoubtedly is in its prolixity; but there is a good case to be made for ranking it among the great novels of the twentieth century.

Yet, for its author, the immediate aftermath of its publication was a sense of failure and, worse, a lawsuit. In August 1932, five months after its initial appearance in America, he noted in his diary that 'only' 4,000 copies had been sold and $780 received 'when three thousand was what we hoped for'.

> This is a Serious Blow to which I must adjust myself when I had been secretly hoping for I know not what terrific Kudos including the Noble [sic] Prize and being knighted by my Sovereign & receiving the acclamation of Europe & seeing the book translated into all languages — & best of all sold at the entrance to the Ruins in Glastonbury itself! Well I must resign myself to its being a failure.
>
> (PATD, 109)

Glastonbury, however, signally failed to take this romance to its heart. Not only were there no sales at the entrance to the ruins, but a local businessman sued the author and his London publishers, The Bodley Head, for libel. Captain Gerard William Hodgkinson believed that he would be identified with Philip Crow, the amoral and disagreeable character who in the novel owns the Wookey Hole caverns. The case was settled out of court, Powys's lawyer expressing his client's 'deep regret'. Its effect was such, however, that more than twenty years later, eight pages were omitted from the chapter entitled 'Wookey Hole' in the Macdonald 1955 edition of the novel. Phyllis Playter was outraged by these legal proceedings but Powys was relieved to get the lawyers off his back; he never quite exorcised the ghost of the small boy who had feared the police might lock him up for throwing a stick into the lake in Osmaston Park. The case left him very short of money, and Penny Smith has shown that a decade later friends such as J.D. Beresford and Theodore Dreiser were contributing towards a fund to help him out financially (*Powys Review* no 9, 11).

By the time the libel action was launched, John Cowper Powys was living in England with Phyllis. The decision to leave America had not been made easily, Phyllis having become accustomed at last to rural life in Columbia County. An old longing, however, had taken possession of her partner: to settle in Wales and 'write something with all those Welsh gods & traditions & magic behind me!' This, he assured her, had been a constant refrain in his life, going back to the time when on Brighton beach he had been an avid reader of Welsh history, grammars and poetry. 'This is a Recurrence of an ancient strain of music, a sort of far off Pilgrims' chorus in my long life,' he wrote lyrically in his diary on 5 September 1933 (PATD, 134). Financial stringency forced them into a decision: they were living beyond their means at Phudd Bottom. He was briefly tempted by the idea of living in Aberystwyth, where the National Library of Wales' store of old Welsh books would help him write his projected romance about Merlin and Taliesin, but when at last they left America on the first day of June 1934 their destination was the county where he had spent so much of his childhood and youth: Dorset.

They settled first in Rat's Barn, an isolated farmhouse on the South Dorset Downs which lived down to its name by being thoroughly primitive. Phyllis here found herself amid a plethora of Powyses, for within a mile or two of each other John's brothers Theodore and Llewelyn, with their respective wives, and sisters Gertrude and Philippa (Katie) were all to be found. John would walk a mile over the downs to read to his favourite brother Llewelyn, who was by then suffering a recurrence of his old enemy, tuberculosis, and spitting blood. Phyllis enjoyed a visit to Weymouth and spoke warmly of the possibility of spending the winter there, a treat that was to be denied her. There was an awkward meeting between John and Littleton, who reproached his elder brother for not telling him about his relationship with Phyllis, but since John's son Littleton Alfred had only found out about it himself a few months earlier he could have had no real quarrel.

By the autumn John and Phyllis had moved again: to Dorchester. They took a flat above a grocer's shop at 38 High East Street, moving in on his sixty-second birthday on 8 October. Phyllis's first shopping expedition included the purchase of a chamber pot, John lying on his bed while she acquired such 'important things'. Back among scenes of his childhood, he enjoyed the sight of the sun rising over Stinsford Brook and slanting on to the spire of All Saints Church. His happiness increased with the release of his beloved dog The Black from quarantine but Phyllis was so miserable that he began to wonder if they had been wise to leave America after all. She had, at least, the consolation of being free from the oppressive proximity of her husband's relations, for the egoism of the Powyses and what she saw as their lack of refinement annoyed her intensely. 'O the little T.T.!' he cried out to his diary on the last day of the year, 'I do hope I can make you happy in my country *ere long*.' But which country was it to be, the England of his birth or the ancestral Wales for which he still felt what many of his siblings regarded as an illogical, even absurd, longing?

The issue was to be settled with surprising swiftness, but in the meantime he was writing as busily as ever. Incredibly, the year of *A Glastonbury Romance's* publication had seen the appearance also in America of his third great Wessex novel *Weymouth Sands*. It would not be published in Britain until 1935 and then only under a different title because, in the wake of the disaster of the *Glastonbury* libel suit, there were fears of fresh legal trouble if another novel were to be placed in a precise location. Powys, who while planning the book in America had scoured street plans of Weymouth to refresh his memory of the town, went to the length of employing a local man to compare his novel with the reality. It was as well that he did so, as it appears that one of his characters, the town clerk 'Sippy' Ballard, bore an uncanny resemblance to an actual official of the borough (TBP, 267).

The novel, which Powys constantly refers to as 'my Weymouth Book' in his diaries, was eventually brought out by John Lane of The Bodley Head under the title *Jobber Skald*, the name of one of its principal characters. It is much shorter than *A Glastonbury Romance* but equally vital and arresting. We are plunged immediately into the life of Magnus Muir, a John Cowper Powys-like figure who awaits the arrival at Weymouth of a steamer from the Channel Islands bringing young Perdita Wane, who is to be companion to the wife of a local celebrity, the famous clown Jerry Cobbold. Muir is a 'tutor in Latin to backward boys,' a less unlikely vocation in the early 1930s than it would be today. He shares many of his creator's neuroses and obsessive anxieties, his personality contrasting sharply with that of Adam Skald, a man of majestic physique who earns a living running his motor-boat between the neighbouring coastal towns.

Weymouth Sands, which was not published in Britain under its proper title until 1963, is not quite so thickly populated as *A Glastonbury Romance*, but it has characters as diverse as the young philosopher Richard Gaul, who is spared the nuisance of earning a living by possessing a small inheritance, the half-crazy orphan boy Larry Zed, the mystic Sylvanus Cobbold (brother of Jerry) and the revolting Dr Brush, who runs a sanatorium for the mentally ill and practises vivisection as a sideline. The critic Glen Cavaliero has observed that the book has 'a distinctive character of its own, a character drawn largely from Powys's feeling for the seaside town which is its setting' (JCPN, 79). Thinly disguised as Sea-Sands in the novel's original incarnation, Weymouth lives and breathes through these pages. There are the 'wet sands' and 'dry sands' where Powys played as a boy when spending holidays with his grandmother at Penn House. There are the donkeys, the Punch and Judy man, the evangelical beach preachers, the cross-Channel steamers disgorging their passengers on to the pier. And there are the unmistakable landmarks of the town itself, notably the Jubilee Clock and the statue of George the Third, which in a vivid passage in the opening chapter undergo a remarkable transformation in Muir's imagination.

> On this occasion that sudden whistle of the Cherbourg steamer produced a very queer impression on his mind. It was an impression as if the whole of Weymouth had suddenly become an insubstantial vapour suspended in space. All the particular aspects of the place known to him so well, the spire of St John's Church, the rounded stucco-facade of Number One Brunswick Terrace and of Number One St Mary's Street, the Jubilee Clock, the Nothe, the statue of George the Third, seemed to emerge gigantically from a mass of vaporous unreality. This hallucination, or whatever it was, lasted a very

> short time. A second blowing of the vessel's whistle dissipated it completely; but not before it had been borne upon him that if he was really such a coward he would have to sink back upon some philosophy that included and completely allowed for such grotesque treacheries.
>
> (WS, 25)

Weymouth Sands displays the weaknesses as well as the strengths of John Cowper Powys in abundance: his failure to structure a novel in such a way as to give the reader a sense of following a coherent story, the strain he places on our credibility both in his characterisation and dialogue. Thus Jobber Skald is impossible to place socially, and characters such as the fishmonger Witchit and his wife tend to speak, like the embarrassingly folksy Number One and Number Two in *A Glastonbury Romance*, in the local-yokel dialect with which Powys encumbers characters outside the middle and upper classes. The truth is that Powys, while thoroughly democratic in outlook and able to enjoy neighbourly accord with people from much poorer backgrounds than his own, found difficulty in capturing both the speech and the sensibilities of working-class people. His triumph is in his ability to create imaginative worlds so powerful that it is possible to accept them on his own terms, substituting his reality for our own while he holds us in his thrall.

For the author himself, the dominant purpose of *Weymouth Sands* was to show the reciprocity that develops between human lives and particular places. 'The book deals in fact with the psychic interplay of spiritual and chemical forces, between nature and men and women, in one particular spot,' he wrote in a magazine article in November 1933. Weymouth was, of all places, 'the one most constantly familiar to me from my earliest infancy.' Through Magnus Muir and Sylvanus Cobbold, 'the left and the right so to speak of my own skeleton,' he had expressed opinions which were 'shockingly out of tune' with the times.

> One of these opinions is a rooted hostility to the practice of vivisection; and the other, intimately connected with this and indeed underlying it, is a profound distrust of almost every aspect of modern science.
>
> Driven, as I meditate upon the subtle interpenetration of human personality and nature, to regard modern science as a menace to so much that is noble, subtle, powerful and

> original in individual character, I have taken the opportunity of having myself projected on this stage — these Weymouth Sands — of my life's dominant background, to indicate how much more important for the happiness of the world is personal character than any scientific knowledge.
>
> (*The Modern Thinker*, November 1933, reprinted in *The Powys Review* no 11)

This was the credo of John Cowper Powys, expressed not only in his novels and philosophical writings but in the manner of his living. To the last he stood opposed to the zeitgeist of the twentieth century, subverting not only its cruelties but, perhaps, something of the malice he detected in the First Cause itself.

Thirteen

In some ways, Dorchester should have been the ideal location for John Cowper Powys. It had old associations with his childhood, and strong literary connections: he had seen the poet William Barnes stroll its shady groves, and enjoyed personal acquaintance with the great Thomas Hardy, who had once gravely inscribed 'Thomas Hardy, a Wayfarer,' in the visitors' book at the Mabelulu Castle, the playhouse erected in the garden of Montacute Vicarage by his younger brothers and sisters. Dorchester was, too, the setting of the new novel which he had already begun writing, and which was to be named after the huge earthwork just outside the town, Maiden Castle. Yet the rooms above the grocer's shop in High East Street were his home for only eight months, for by the end of May the following year he and Phyllis had gone to live in Wales, and there they remained.

The move was so creative an act, a working out of one of his deepest personal mythologies, that it is apt that it should have been assisted by a fellow novelist, James Hanley. Hanley, a much younger writer than John Cowper Powys, had settled in Wales with his wife to write novels bristling with social realism, many of them inspired by his unhappy experiences as a merchant seaman. (His novel *Boy* was a cause célèbre in the 1930s, being withdrawn after the publishers were convicted of obscene libel; it was not re-published in full until 1990.) It was the Hanleys who found John and Phyllis their first home in Wales, close to where they themselves lived in the small village of Cynwyd, just outside Corwen in the county of Merioneth. Nothing could have been less pretentious, for it was a furnished wooden bungalow which, according to James Hanley, belonged to a Welsh gipsy. Noting in his diary that they had taken the bungalow from 17 May 1935, Powys added that he had just been reading of a battle fought in Corwen between the sons of the Welsh prince

Llewelyn the Great. For some weeks, in fact, he had been immersing himself in Welsh history preparatory to the move: 'We keep reading over and over again about Llangollen and Dinas Bran and Owain Glendwr [sic] and Madoc ap Griffith the Discoverer of America,' reads his diary entry for 17 April.

On his last morning in Dorchester, Powys rose at six, slowly shaved and prepared for the arrival of the Great Western Railway lorry for their luggage. The driver was so 'very nice' that he twice gave him two shillings, although he does not explain whether this was a mistake or deliberate generosity. Train tickets were needed not only for themselves but for their dog, which was variously known as The Black, The Old Black or simply The Old. The sense of returning to ancestral places was clearly uppermost in Powys's mind, for he and Phyllis broke their journey by staying in Ludlow overnight on 19 May and taking a taxi to the Shropshire village of Bitterley to visit the graves of Powys ancestors. The following afternoon they arrived in Wales, 'the land of my fathers,' Powys noted, making the acquaintance of the 'charming Mrs Cadwallader, who is as beautiful as she is kind and competent,' and who made tea at their new home for themselves and James Hanley. Powys evidently had some misconceptions about life in Wales, as going into the village next morning he attempted to speak to Mrs Evans the Grocer in sign language, imagining that all Welsh people spoke only Welsh. 'This performance was an astonishment to the good lady who assumed that a Madman, led by a Black Dog, was arrived in Cynwyd. However, she replied in perfectly good English,' he noted.

Powys appears to have happily embraced life in Cynwyd from the outset, thanking 'the Spirit of my Mother for the happiness of this place' and even eating vegetables and cheese and drinking beer 'for the first time for years'. Phyllis, however, was predictably cast down, being averse to having someone else's furniture around her. A few days after their arrival she declared that she no longer cared for nature or the picturesque but craved for life in a metropolis like Paris or London. When he replied that he would far sooner live in a city where she would be happy than anywhere else, however, she cried that 'just as I hate to sacrifice her so she hates to sacrifice me and there we are!' Illuminatingly he added that Dorchester had been a compromise which had been satisfying to neither.

After a 'heavenly day' in Bala he rhapsodised on the beauty of the Welsh language and the following day Phyllis joined him on an early morning walk, something she had never done before. The move into the furnished bungalow was obviously intended to be only a temporary measure, as the Powyses were already looking at other houses. After turning down 'a tiny little fairy cottage' (but damp), they visited Cae Coed, a row of semi-detached houses in Corwen newly built by a local landowner, Admiral Cotton. These appealed to them so much that they 'boldly visited the Admiral his wone self' and told him they wanted number seven. It was theirs for the taking at 12s 6d a week rent including rates, and it remained their home for twenty years.

They did not actually move in until July, and in the meantime Powys took a train to Worcester to visit his son, booking rooms for them both at the Star Inn. It is curiously touching to find him drawing significance from the fact that Littleton Alfred felt relaxed enough to take a nap in the hotel lounge, 'for I cannot imagine myself daring to retire to rest from the presence of *my* father!'

For all the upheaval of house removal, John Cowper Powys continued steadily with his writing. He had completed two more non-fiction books, *A Philosophy of Solitude* and *The Art of Happiness*, against the advice of Phyllis, who thought he should confine himself to novels. She dismissed them as 'hurried little tracts for the times' and 'pigeon roost sermons' and he sometimes appears to have had little regard for them himself, referring to his 'little wretched *Philosophy of Solitude*'. They were, however, a useful source of income and it is important to remember that authors are often inclined to say worse things about their own writing than they really mean. He certainly felt that his happiness book might help people teased by the sort of 'mental obstacles' which he understood so well, and the fact that these tracts were written to tight deadlines was not itself a source of worry. He confessed that he tended 'to write better sometimes in a rush ... I have to get started like a telegraph wire in the wind & then when the wind gathers to a rush the tune emerges!'

All such works were, however, of little significance to him beside his novels. Now at the height of his creative powers, he had thrown himself into his latest, *Maiden Castle*, with enthusiasm. His sense of parallel worlds is at the heart of his philosophy, and it is expressed in this novel in the obsession of one of its characters, Enoch Quirm, with the remote past and its relevance to the world of today. Quirm, a man of Welsh origin who has given himself the name of Uryen, is trying to get in touch with the old gods of Mai-Dun, another name for Maiden Castle, believing there to have been a Golden Age which had a power existing still in this huge neolithic earthwork. In a climactic scene he expresses his sense of its immediacy and the possibility that it might yet break through to 'explode forever the superstition of science'. Through Quirm, Powys gives the Welsh word 'hiraeth', which usually expresses intense longing or nostalgia, a new and more positive meaning.

> If John Rhys were alive I'd have left you all, years ago, and gone to tell *him* the whole thing. He'd have understood, for he put me on the track of it. *He* knew how all Taliesin's prophecies were about me. He knew how all the old bards worshipped what works through me. *He* knew the mysterious secret of my race, of *his* race; that straining, that longing, that yearning for it — no other tongue has a word like that! — and *he* knew what it meant. Desire, but not ordinary desire. Desire grown beside itself! Desire driven against custom, driven against habit, driven against the cowardice of mankind ... That's what *Hiraeth* is!
>
> (MC, 467)

It is possible to react strongly against such outbursts as mere hokum, Powysian romanticism run riot, but in so doing one would reject something of the essence of John Cowper Powys's belief in the unreality of time, as usually conceived. Remote past and distant future, he would say, co-exist in our own personalities; the old gods our ancestors worshipped and the superhuman race that will inherit the earth are as one; and this knowledge, once grasped, has a redemptive power that transcends the niggling worries to which we are prone in our small, circumscribed lives.

Quirm, however, is not the central character in a novel which, for all the vigour with which ideas are expressed, comes as something of a disappointment. This is partly due to the fact that its anti-hero, the absurdly-named Dud No-Man, bears too close a resemblance to John Cowper Powys himself for comfort. This self-obsession seems lazy and regressive, signifying perhaps too great a haste in embarking on another Wessex novel. Dud, like Powys, lives in High East Street, Dorchester, listening to all the early morning sounds in a way that echoes entries in the diaries. It is possible, of course, to see too much of Powys in Dud, yet light is surely thrown on the author's marital difficulties as a young man in Dud's reflections on the wife, now dead, whom he failed to satisfy sexually.

> It was not that he had ever loved her ... with a normal love, for it was Dud's misfortune to be rendered nervously incapable of consummating his marriage, but his bride's startling beauty and singular character had made a deeper impression upon him than anything in his life; and for all these ten years Mona's personality had stood between him and all other emotional impressions. Now that it was too late, now that she had died a virgin, the vision of that beautiful body, ready to yield itself and yet so terrifyingly immaculate, had come to absorb every amorous instinct he possessed.
>
> All feelings of that sort, such as now and then were stirred in him by casual encounters, invariably ran, like subservient tributaries, into this main stream. The glimpse of a lovely ankle, the turn of a soft neck, the swing of a girl's figure as she walked, if such things were ever dwelt upon in his thoughts, were always caught up and transformed in his memory to make part of his enjoyment of that terrifyingly beautiful body.
>
> (MC, 20)

There is something dangerously close to a parodying of Thomas Hardy's Dorchester novel, *The Mayor of Casterbridge*, in the fact that Dud buys a wife, the circus-girl Wizzie Ravelson, who with her wild impetuosity and bloody-minded independence is one of the best-drawn characters. Not surprisingly, she leaves the neurotic Dud, who at the last contemplates existence with Wolf Solent-like resignation.

> 'Hold to the centre,' he said to himself, 'as you move on. The future's *not* everything.' And he dug his stick into the earth, with his eyes on the ground. Then, pulling it out with a jerk, he went to meet Nance.
>
> (MC, 496)

In its unequivocal matter-of-factness, this rivals the conclusion of *Wolf Solent*.

> 'I wonder if he *is* still here?' he thought as he laid his hand on the latch of the gate. And then he thought. 'Well, I shall have a cup of tea.'
>
> (WoS, 614)

It is as if Powys is reminding us that, for all the grandeur of our speculations, life must be sustained first and foremost on a humble level.

The extraordinary productivity of the years immediately following his retirement from lecturing is emphasised by the fact that he found time to write not only his major Wessex novels and 'tracts for the times' but his immense *Autobiography*, in some ways his most remarkable book of all. In fact, it can almost be regarded as a novel itself, so enthralling a narrative does it provide. In its breathtaking frankness and almost insolent disregard for the effect his confessions of personal weakness might have on the reader, it has a Rousseau-like sublimity. But it stands alone in one respect: women are almost entirely excluded from its pages. It was his intention to exclude them altogether, but to shut out half the human race from his life story proved impossible even for his genius. The women we find here, however, share an almost complete anonymity. They exist as 'street-girls' with whom he had fleeting sexual adventures, 'shoals of schoolgirls' in Brighton, divine possessors of exquisite ankles which he admired from afar (or near), rich women aboard Atlantic liners, members of ladies' clubs to whom he lectured in America. All (with the possible exception of Lily, the prostitute whom he invited home to Burpham), were of no importance to him whatever. The women of consequence: his mother, his sisters, his wife Margaret, Frances Gregg, Phyllis Playter: all are snuffed out as though they never existed. This makes *Autobiography*, for all its power and candour, a curiously distorted account of himself. His stated aim was to avoid hurting people, but there was hurt enough for Margaret in these accounts of his sterile lusting after sylph-like creatures in the early days of their marriage, his sad encounters with prostitutes and the excitement provided by the company of Tom Jones's 'sweet-natured women' in Liverpool. At the core of *Autobiography* is a shuffling evasiveness, a refusal to acknowledge failures far more profound than any he confesses in these tumbling, highly-coloured pages. Most of all, one suspects, it was the ruin of his marriage that forced him into making *Autobiography* a book written on what he called 'a very singular method ... *No Women at all* — not even my Mother'. His abandonment of Margaret in all but a financial sense, the sexual inadequacy which his marriage so cruelly exposed, lay like a stone at the heart of him. Once Margaret was excised, so must all the others be. It was, indeed, an autobiography 'such as has never been writ before,' as he informed his sister Marian, but its uniqueness stands as indictment as well as triumph.

The book was written at breakneck speed and published in 1934, the year John Cowper Powys left America with Phyllis Playter. For all the criticism ventured here, *Autobiography* is a hugely enjoyable work, teeming with life and incident. If the author fails to reveal all, he reveals far more than is usual. Inevitably, anyone attempting to write a life of John Cowper Powys must draw on it liberally. It tells us not only about himself but about the times in which he lived, not as revealed in great public events but in his own day-to-day living. This took in so many places and such a diversity of humanity that it makes a rich feast. At its conclusion, he felt that it had taken him half a century 'merely to learn with what weapons, and with what surrender of weapons, *I am to begin to live my life*'.

To pass one's sixtieth birthday and still to feel that life is only just beginning is indeed to tempt Providence. But in this case the First Cause turned its malignancy aside, allowing this troublesome human insect nearly thirty years more on the planet; and all but one of them spent in Wales.

Fourteen

John Cowper Powys soon became a familiar figure in Corwen, walking the streets of the small town or the surrounding countryside, stout walking-stick invariably in hand. His enthusiasm for Wales even persuaded him to argue that Welsh rain was less malign than the Dorset variety, which 'drenches you to the skin,' whereas Welsh rain was more diffused — 'misty rain, mountain-mist rain, soft vaporous rain, rain that is really *entering into a cloud....*' There was a pleasant surprise of a different kind when he found that the man delivering parcels from the railway station was able to speak intelligently about Welsh poetry of the ninth century. 'Think of an English labourer talking about Beowulf!' he exclaimed admiringly.

Everything was of intense interest to him, not least the way the local sheep were able to bound goat-like up the mountain rocks. He saw plenty of them, for Cae Coed was on a slope of the Berwyns where he took daily walks with his spaniel. He would set off very early, gazing down the valley of the Dee with its romantic associations with Owain Glyndwr. There were inevitable difficulties in adjusting to this new way of life, but the Hanleys helped to smooth their path and so did a neighbour whom Powys identified as 'Mr Edmonds from South Wales,' who had accompanied them in viewing other houses before they decided on the one in Cae Coed.

The unassuming interest in cultural matters which Powys discovered in the people of Corwen was a constant delight. It meant a far wider circle of friends (or at least friendly acquaintances) than ever before, strengthening his concept of the Welsh as belonging to a much older and wiser race than the English. These relationships were sometimes fortuitously struck, one such being with the family of a local men's outfitter, John Morgan. On his first visit to the shop Powys wrote out a cheque and, seeing the signature, Morgan remarked that it was 'a well-known name'. Powys's surprise at being recognised led to an animated conversation and the beginning of a lasting friendship.

Morgan's wife was the Welsh language novelist Elena Puw Morgan, but it is through their daughter Catrin, then a child, that some impressions of John Cowper Powys and Phyllis Playter in Corwen have come down to the writer of this biography. Mrs Catrin Puw Davies recalled:

> What I want to say first of all is that Mr Powys was a very nice man. He was a most striking-looking person, very tall and with a mop of curls and piercing eyes. Phyllis Playter was known to everyone as Mrs Powys. They never tried to hide the fact that they weren't married, and she always signed herself Playter, but people thought that was because they were arty types.
>
> My parents were always afraid of imposing themselves on them so they didn't go to their house as often as they were invited, but they came to our house almost daily. Mrs Powys would come down with a huge shopping basket on her arm like a farmer's wife and he used to come too. They were very friendly because my parents were very well-read. Mr Powys was very keen to know Welsh and to try to learn it but he had no gift for languages so couldn't speak it at all. In the early days he did try, but people couldn't understand what he was saying so he gave up.
>
> They had bookcases everywhere in their house, with rows of Welsh books, particularly *The Mabinogion* and things like that. He was thrilled with mythology. Whenever he had visitors he brought them to our house, and my mother would often invite them for a meal. I'm sure it was because he wanted them to meet a Welsh family. His two brothers came to our house, Theodore and Llewelyn. I don't remember them as writers, only as friends of my parents.
>
> Mr Powys had a very peculiar diet, mostly mouldy bread and raw eggs. They would buy loaves and put them on a shelf in the kitchen until they became mouldy enough for him to eat. You would see this long row of loaves, in increasing stages of mouldiness. I can remember seeing Mrs Powys crack an egg into a glass for him. It made me feel quite sick, he would just swallow it. I used to hate to see him swallowing an egg like that.
>
> When they invited us to their house they gave us a very nice conventional tea. I used to like seeing his walking sticks; they had animal heads carved on them and were all in a stand in the hall. Upstairs in his study he used to keep a death mask,

and I didn't like that at all. Mrs Powys once gave me a little Japanese doll, and some big photographs of churches in Brittany.

All the tramps used to call at their house and he had long conversations with them. I remember the time Mrs Powys bought him a new overcoat and he gave it away to a tramp. She was furious. There was a great search, everyone was scouring the countryside looking for this tramp with his new coat; I think they got it back in the end. He made friends with people living in the slums of Corwen; he'd give them money when he didn't have enough to heat his own house properly.

He used to get up very early for his long walk up the mountain, setting off up the lane that went past his house. When he went walking he wore corduroy trousers and an old jacket, very threadbare. This walk would last hours because he would worship stones and trees on the way and commune with nature. I remember going for a walk with my parents and coming across all these twigs in strange shapes, left like that by Mr Powys. When I picked them up my mother shouted, 'Put them down or Mr Powys will think the end of the world has come.' She thought he would see it as a portent. He put them down to mark places that were special to him.

When my father went in hospital, Mr Powys wrote him a letter saying that on the morning of the operation he would go to worship before his most special tree. He would walk around the tree twelve times and call upon the most potent spirits and my father would be alright because this would see him through the operation. A lot of people thought him odd but my parents didn't. Oh they liked him, he was such a good man. You felt that he was full of goodness.

This generous view of John Cowper Powys is typical of the reactions he inspired among the Welsh people he came to know during the final period of his life. They responded not only to his stature as a writer but to his openness and vivacity, the child-like way he would clap his hands excitedly during conversation and his absolute lack of pomposity. He had an uncanny knack of making people aware of their own potential, drawing them out in such a way that their self-belief was enhanced tenfold. 'He could see what you were at your greatest,' said Oliver Marlow Wilkinson. 'There would be showers of sparks around your head. He would tell you that you could achieve all you wished in such a way that you would go away believing you could.' This trait was capable of being satirised in such a way that it could appear mere flattery, as in Louis (Marlow) Wilkinson's brutal depiction of the young Powys in the guise of Jack Welsh in his satirical novel *The Buffoon*.

> 'Capital!' Welsh hugged himself. 'Nothing could please me better. What a situation! A master! You are indeed! You are a master! .... How well you can deal with things, Mr Raynes! .... Upon my word I admire you. I admire you!'
>
> His tone was almost servile. Edward suspected in him a mania for placating people. Was it that Welsh felt unable to 'deal with them' in any other way?
>
> (TB, 34)

Powys's need to 'propitiate' was certainly endemic in him, and in many of his fictional characters. This avoidance of open conflict was possibly rooted in the unhappiness of his schooldays in Sherborne, and an even deeper unhappiness in early childhood. His relationship with his father was ambiguous, love and respect being mixed with awe and fear of a strong and authoritarian parent. His interest in other people, however, and his instinctive sympathy for tramps and derelicts made the mature John Cowper Powys a fascinating and alluring figure. Gilbert Turner, a librarian who visited him in Corwen, has noted his 'endearing trait' of being ready to 'listen to all the misfits, or as he used to call them, "funny ones," so that Cae Coed became a kind of sanctuary and refuge where these people could be sure of a sympathetic hearing.'

> This readiness to listen to all manner of unlikely people was, as I am sure everyone who met him must agree, accompanied by an ability to draw you out, giving the impression that you were the most important person in his life and that he had been waiting only for the supreme pleasure of talking to you. I have seen shy and diffident visitors, especially young people, encouraged into a hitherto completely unknown loquacity.
>
> (ROTBP, 217)

The voluminous correspondence which Powys kept up with a wide assortment of people is further proof of the selfless giving of himself which he found inescapable. It took up several hours of the day and might be regarded as wasteful of the time and energy of an ageing writer who could ill afford to squander either, yet while often impatient with the demands it made on him he felt bound to answer all letters fully. He was incapable of dashing off stock phrases but made every letter personal, whether the correspondent was known to him or not. The result is the existence of thousands of letters, in each of which the authentic voice of John Cowper Powys rings out. Like his diaries, they are bespattered with exclamation marks and underlinings, and any one of them might contain confessions of the most intimate nature. 'I have a *horror* of "fucking" as it is called,' he wrote to Glyn Hughes from Blaenau Ffestiniog in 1957. 'It is amazing how I ever managed to have a son!' Hughes, then twenty-five, had first written to Powys only three months previously, expressing admiration for his work and seeking his advice. A man of varied occupation, including film extra and circus musician, he found himself the fortunate recipient of more than thirty letters from Powys over the next four years, extracts from which were later published.

Another regular correspondent was Benson Roberts, who combined the trade of grocer in the Glamorgan market town of Bridgend with a keen appreciation of literature: the kind of quirky combination in which John Cowper Powys delighted. In October 1938 he invited Powys to give a lecture on the suggestion of Gerard Casey, who was later to marry Mary Penny, daughter of Lucy, youngest daughter of Charles Francis and Mary Cowper Powys. 'Yes I am indeed happy and proud to be coming to give a lecture in Bridgend,' Powys enthused in his reply, to Roberts's delight. 'I hasten to confirm and cordially agree to everything you say in your letter about the date, Monday Dec 5th and subject — "The First Four Books of the Mabinogion" — and the fee inclusive of ten guineas.' This would, he added, be his first freelance paid lecture in the land of his fathers — 'for I don't count my early Univ. Extens. lectures as *either* of those things — for *they* were just as alien to Wales as The Archbishop of Canterbury!' (LTBR, 15).

Powys declined an invitation to stay longer in Bridgend because of the strict diet which he had been maintaining for the past seven years. During that time, he confessed, he had failed to have a natural action of the bowels but relied on 'a particular sort of American *Enema* which I can only get here at home'. It was, in fact, administered by Phyllis, whose elderly mother and aunt were now living next to them in Corwen. Powys referred to their 'little American Colony in Cae Coed' in a further letter to Benson Roberts after giving the lecture, 'an ageing Clown of the Platform who was perhaps over-intoxicated to smell the familiar saw-dust of the Circus again.'

This was the first of two lectures which Powys gave in Bridgend. They brought him into contact with the poet Huw Menai, a former colliery checkweighman now on the dole. The two men struck up an instant friendship, Powys effusively hailing Menai as the greatest personality he had met, with the sole exception of Thomas Hardy. Around this time Powys also made contact with the Welsh scholar Iorwerth Peate, who became curator of the Welsh National Folk Museum at St Fagans, just outside Cardiff. He had, in fact, fired off a letter to him (boldly written in Welsh with the aid of a dictionary) when he first received the invitation to lecture in Bridgend, asking if a further lecture might be arranged for the following day in Cardiff. 'This I would never have done if I'd known the two places were near enough to you to be able to draw on Cardiff for your audience,' he confessed to Benson Roberts.

The letter, though ill-conceived, forged the first link in yet another chain of correspondence, Peate responding warmly to Powys's keen interest in Welsh letters. The cultural establishment of Wales, in fact, gave John Cowper Powys the kind of acceptance that escaped him in England, the University of Wales bestowing on him an honorary doctorate of literature in 1962, the year before his death. It is a matter for shame that, for all his achievements, this was one of only two high academic honours awarded him, the other being the Bronze Plaque for 'outstanding services to literature and philosophy' given by the Hamburg Free Academy of Arts in 1958.

In May 1936, within a year of his migration into Wales, the region which he identified as his ancestral home had paid its own homage. The Powys Eisteddfod, an annual event staged that year in Corwen, made him a bard. It was, he declared, 'an extraordinarily thrilling event in our life,' coinciding with Phyllis's birthday, 'a day which is more important to her than any other day.' John's sister Katie, staying with them in Cae Coed, was delighted to hear the band play the stirring march *Men of Harlech* (a favourite of hers) and to see the eisteddfod proclaimed in grand manner. Characteristically, the Horn of Plenty reminded her eldest brother of Ceridwen's Cauldron, soaked as he was now in all the richness of Welsh legend. Unhappily the heavens opened but John Cowper Powys emerged from the ceremony with the bardic name of Ioan Powys, something he could not have foretold when his first slim volume had shyly made its appearance forty years previously.

The transition from upstate New York to Merioneth, via the staging post of Dorchester, could not have been easy, especially for Phyllis. But for the complex and driven man with whom she had united herself, this was an unavoidable destiny.

> Why did I come to live in Wales? Why did I thus isolate myself, so far from my brothers and sisters? Not, I think, from my mania for solitude and independence, but as the fulfilment of an early and youthful longing — 'hiraeth' is the Welsh word for this obscure stirring of some secret destiny — to return to the land of my remote ancestors.
> (OC, 55)

Corwen responded to his acute sense of antiquity. From his house in Cae Coed he could not only look down the pastoral valley of the Dee but across to a hill fort that stirred his imagination. The churchyard half a mile away held a strange old pillar with carvings he associated with the cult of the Earth-Mother in Crete a millennium ago. And, a mere afternoon's bus-ride away, a yet more ancient pillar stood, commemorating a king of the region named Eliseg.

> This monument to King Eliseg stands on a burial-mound within a few hundred yards of the ruins of Valle Crucis Abbey and never — not even at Glastonbury — have I felt the spirit of what Spengler would call the Spring-time of our Faustian Culture as powerfully as in this holy ground. The thirteenth century Cistercian chapter-house remains entirely intact, and it would be easily possible to make use of this scholastic sanctuary in the mountains not only for Thibetan contemplation but for the writing of books.
>
> Here was buried the famous family-bard of Owen Glendower, Iolo Goch, and here is the tomb of the love-lorn Myfanwy, a Princess from the embattled hill-castle of the chiefs of this region, known as Dinas Bran.
>
> The ruins of Dinas Bran tower up, jagged and desolate above the romantic town of Llangollen; and to initiates in Welsh mythology it is of Bran the Blessed, one of the most singular of the ancient gods who became either saints or devils in the christian era, rather than of the flocks of black-winged birds — though Bran means a crow — that still hover round it, that this wild fortress must speak. Bards and Gods and Demons and Druids have all left indelible impressions on the landscape of my new home ...
> (OC, 56)

Eliseg, Valle Crucis, Dinas Bran; all three played a part in the new romance which Powys began writing in the spring of 1937. For some, Owen Glendower is a work that puts him in the front rank of historical novelists; for others, it is so careless of historical fact as to be irredeemably flawed. It is one of the two major novels which he wrote while living in Wales, and whatever its merits or defects, it is highly revealing not only of his attitude to Wales but of his own perception of time and external reality.

Fifteen

For John Cowper Powys, the past was not impossibly distant but something contemporary, co-existing with present and future in a timeless dimension which could be imaginatively entered. This belief enabled him to give his great historical romances, *Owen Glendower* and *Porius*, a startling immediacy. The reader is transported not so much into remote times as into parallel worlds in which people speak in exactly the way we do ourselves and react much as we do to innovation. There are obvious advantages in this for the author. The problem of conveying antiquated forms of speech is overcome, and the difficulty of interpreting a different set of values and a world view entirely foreign to ourselves does not exist. Whether historical truth is served is another matter.

Debate of this kind inevitably attends criticism of Powys's works, none more so than the two major novels he wrote while living in Wales. Both *Owen Glendower* and *Porius* have a grandeur of concept which is breathtaking and humbling. The former deals with the uprising against English rule early in the fifteenth century led by Owain Glyndwr, whereas the latter is set in the year 499. Not the least impressive thing about them is their size: *Porius* is a 'buggerly great book' (his own description) of around 500,000 words, while he precisely estimated the length of *Owen Glendower* as 336,856 words. This is eloquent testimony to the sheer creative energy of an author physically nourished by a skimpy diet of raw eggs, milk and stale bread, an author who, in his own view, was 'a permanent invalid — though a very strong, very lively invalid!' Writing at breakneck pace, with pen and ink on a writing pad resting against his knees as he sat propped up on a couch, he was a man inspired. His visions are dazzling, sometimes lurid, his words tumultuous and unsparing. Much of the action in *Owen Glendower* takes place in enclosed spaces, castles and abbeys and palaces where people debate and argue great issues or the small domestic concerns that make up the greater part of life. The book is evidence of the colossal nerve and supreme self-confidence of a writer who feels the past is his to command and reshape. It is a Powysian past, made of the stuff of his genius. This is not to say that his knowledge of the era is flimsy; quite the opposite. The Argument he appends to the novel shows an awesome grasp of the historical context of the Glyndwr adventure. It is the use to which he puts his knowledge that is questionable. Some Welsh scholars, notably Roland Mathias, have seen a lack of political credibility in the novel. 'It is a pity that John Cowper Powys, for all his gifts,' writes Mathias, 'should have decided to tackle a subject so intrinsically concerned with the nature and the making of a *Prince*, and yet to circumvent history, against all credibility, with a formula of his own. He might have done better with the cliché of Shakespeare's wizard' (EAJCP, 261).

One of the most controversial aspects of the book is the personality of Owen himself. He is clearly visualised as a tall man with a yellow-grey beard and eyes of 'a flickering sea-colour, sometimes grey and sometimes green,' his forehead low and broad, his nose Roman, with unnaturally large nostrils. His cheek-bones are prominent, his cheeks 'hollow and curiously white against his yellow-grey hair,' his skin freckled rather than tanned by exposure to the elements. He has a courtly manner towards his guests, speaking in a voice so low that only the person addressed could hear what he was saying. There is nothing in this imaginative reconstruction to offend, but as we get to know Owen better we find disturbing hints of other Powys heroes or anti-heroes, traces in fact of John Cowper Powys himself. This Glendower (only occasionally does Powys refer to him as Owain Glyn Dwr) is introspective and neurotic, plagued with doubt even as he is declared Prince of Wales.

> 'Long live Owen, Prince of Powys!'
> 'Blood,' he said to himself. 'Blood and ashes! That's what *this* means.'
> 'Long live Owen, Prince of Gwynedd!'
> 'I'll do it,' he thought. 'Nothing can stop me now. *But to what end*? There won't be a castle in Wales in Harry's hands when I've finished with him. *But to what end*?'
> (OG, 395)

Rather disconcertingly, Owen reflects soon afterwards that 'it'll mean mumming and miming and play-acting and masquerading, till a man's heart turns sick!' Is this the warrior-prince who had the charisma to unite all Wales to his cause, the visionary who planned the universities which his country would not achieve in reality for nearly five centuries? Even these, it seems, were someone else's idea. After the initial attack on Ruthin that began the Welsh revolution, Powys's Glendower broods, in his Snowdon fastness, on his own limitations.

> 'I shall turn them [the English] out,' he thought. 'Ffraid ferch Gloyw said that; and I've never doubted it. But when it comes to the Universities — and this Lollard says there must be two of 'em, a southern one and a northern — I don't know what to think! English Alfred had the genius of a commander *and* the learning of a monk; but who am I, who get so elated with triumph when I come back from a raid with fifty ponies' worth of plunder! — Good Lord, Universities! There's a vein in you, *Owen the Irresponsible*, that's better adapted to burning markets and storming castles and making princes' courts on the slopes of Snowdon than to the founding of Universities!
> (OG, 448)

There are those who would see this as playing hop-scotch with history, just as Squire Urquhart believed the unfortunate Redfern had played hop-scotch with his History of Dorset. It is, however, a very human Glendower that Powys gives us, neither a cartoon-strip Superman nor a Shakespearian bombast whose claims to wizardry spur Hotspur to raillery.

> Glendower: I can call spirits from the vasty deep.
> Hotspur: Why, so can I, and so can any man;
> But will they come when you do call for them?
> (*King Henry IV — Part One*)

A sense of contemporaneousness is ever-present in *Owen Glendower*. We are in a world of change, like our own, where new ideas and inventions challenge old ways of thought and action. Warfare has altered radically with the introduction of murderous long-bows, far more destructive than the yew-tree bows of old, new buildings are flamboyant with heavy Norman arches and chimneys that carry the smoke away, and Owen's choice of clothes is dictated by fashion: he pulls on silken hose and 'new-fashioned deer-skin garters'. The

Church has little power in these 'degenerate days' and rationalism is brought to bear on occult superstitions. Cynicism is in the air; 'modern cynicism that spoils the romance of everything.'

Glen Cavaliero has observed that this novel, 'like Powys's whole output, is a corrective to false notions about the nature of modernity' (JCPN, 107). He adds that in their interior monologues and reactions the characters are more Powysian than fifteenth century; 'but this is only to pinpoint the fact that Powys is using the fifteenth century, just as he used "contemporary" Glastonbury or Dorchester, to present his own picture of human existence and its dilemmas. His use of the past is functional, not merely informative or aesthetic.'

Anyone bold enough to attempt a novel about Owain Glyndwr, especially a novel of this size and scale, obviously leaves himself open to criticism of the sharpest kind. He is dealing not only with historical fact but myth, for in the Welsh imagination Glyndwr has become like a combination of King Arthur and the wizard Merlin. At the end Glendower, his briefly independent Wales crushed and his fighting days long over, lives out his last days amid the Powys-Fadog hills of his ancestors, betrayed by no-one. John Cowper Powys imposes upon the situation his own philosophy of 'sinking into one's soul'.

> The very geography of the land and its climatic peculiarities, the very nature of its mountains and rivers, the very falling and lifting of the mists that waver above them, all lend themselves, to a degree unknown in any other earthly region, to what might be called the *mythology of escape.* This is the secret of the land. This is the secret of the people of the land. Other races love and hate, conquer and are conquered. This race avoids and evades, pursues and is pursued. Its soul is forever making a double flight. It flees into a circuitous *Inward*. It retreats into a circuitous *Outward*.
>
> You cannot force it to love you or to hate you. You can only watch it escaping from you. Alone among nations it builds no monuments to its princes, no tombs to its prophets. Its past is its future, for it lives by memories and in advance it recedes. The greatest of its heroes have no graves, for they will come again. Indeed they have not died; they have only disappeared. They have only ceased for a while from hunting and being hunted; ceased for a while from their 'longing' that the world which *is* should be transformed into Annwn — the world which *is not* — and yet was and shall be!
>
> (OG, 889)

Whatever liberties it takes with historical truth, *Owen Glendower* is a stupendous novel in which the sights, sounds and smells of early fifteenth century Wales are vividly evoked. Powys effortlessly takes us into his imagined world, in which people who actually existed, such as the warrior Davy Gam, co-exist with invented characters of immense variety. Powys happily splashes around in this sea of action, listening to priests dispute obscure theological points or observing ranks of archers itchily plucking the strings of their engines of death. It was a novel close to his heart, and it shows. He began writing it in the Chapter House amid the ruins of Valle Crucis Abbey, near Llangollen, for he believed that insight into the past can be obtained from absorbing the atmosphere of ancient places. He would have ended it there too, two years and eight months later, but by then it was December 1939 and he did not know how they would get there in the black-out. Instead he climbed to the top of Mynydd y Gaer near his home in Corwen, on Christmas Eve, carrying pen, ink and paper to where he imagined Owain's body being cremated.

> Just as I finished writing with my back to the East — and South — *and my face to the North* — I felt the wind behind me South-East and suddenly over my shoulder into the stone chamber shot a ray of sunlight from the risen sun & made a piece of white *crystal* — that *quartz* — gleam like a diamond.
> (PATD, 333)

The last years of the uneasy peace that separated the two world wars of the twentieth century saw John Cowper Powys reflecting grimly on events in his diaries. 'When I think of Mr Ffoukes Jones' tales of the *last war*,' he wrote on 29 December 1938, 'I sometimes feel as if old Chamberlain were right; and that *peace with dishonour*, which was always what extreme pacifists have believed in, is the old [sic] way to keep the general catastrophe from falling on us!' He continued:

> The dictators well know that we ordinary people feel it is the old, the *only way* — just yielding to their Black-Mail in fear of worse so they go on — But think of the callousness of their black hearts; to risk all this slaughter for such small advantages got by their blackmailing!
> (NLW Ms)

Throughout 1939 he felt the conflict within him between 'feeling and reason' and wondered until the last whether Neville Chamberlain — 'this astonishing old gentleman who obstinately adheres in spite of all to PEACE' — might stop the war after all. He had reflected (not unkindly) on Chamberlain's 'fanaticism for peace' but argued fiercely with Benson Roberts on the Christian basis for pacifism. In a letter of October 1939, he told Roberts that he thought all Jesus's words about returning good for evil and turning the other cheek 'refer to our private affairs with each other'. He repeated the well-worn comment, beloved of muscular Christians, that Jesus 'never told the Centurion that he must leave the army' and argued that Christians could kill in a war and yet remain saintly.

> Pardon my dearest Ben this violent language but Oh dearie I! if you could read some of the letters I get! God! I think this *Above the Melee* attitude is an unworthy one and very unfair to the poor simple devils who have to die that *we* the intelligentsia may have the *right to be pacifists*; as we certainly *would not have* if Hitler wins! We'd *have* to march and drill *then*; or go in concentration camp of sadists! No, no! This is an Historic crisis in the history of the world ... and my own attitude to it — though I tell you my dear Ben I hold my tongue about my contradictory feelings with young people *under* [sic] *military age* — for I think it's *wicked* and most certainly 'un-christian' to push young men into the ranks to fight and perish that we old ones can go on with our damned Art of Happiness! (or any other 'art') without being shot by Hitler or any other Dictator. (LTBR, 33)

This uncompromising support of the war is in striking contrast to the doubts he had expressed the previous year, but is consistent with his general attitude to warfare. Although he had not fought in the Great War he had offered himself for military service, and as the Second World War progressed he propounded with gusto to his friend Louis Wilkinson his theory that with airmen bombing the enemy and ships cannonading them no military offensive might be needed at all. All this may disappoint those who would expect a more ambivalent attitude towards the great moral question of our time (total warfare) on the part of a man who professed to hate cruelty. He could be morbidly sensitive to the feelings which he imagined trees and plants to possess: Llewelyn Powys would recall an occasion when he refused to sit with him on a grassy bank for fear of hurting the vegetation. 'I have *only one* very very very strong principle, conviction, or moral opinion,' he wrote to Louis Wilkinson in 1946, 'namely that Vivisection should be abolished.' In considering John Cowper Powys's protean stance on moral questions, one is irresistibly reminded of Oliver Marlow Wilkinson's remark that he was 'like something out of the earth'. He responded with instinctive outrage to cruelty inflicted on beasts, dismissing as casuistry arguments that laboratory experiments of this kind might save human life or lessen human suffering. The cruelty of war, on the other hand, he was able to justify by maintaining that if the cause were just, the greater good might be served.

Powys's sense of outrage at man's inhumanity to beast was expressed at its fiercest in *Morwyn*, an extended tract against vivisection which with mistaken judgement he thought the best thing he had ever written. Of all his writings, he declared, this would be the one he would single out as the most worthy of survival. In terms of chronology it falls between *Maiden Castle* and *Owen Glendower*, for he began it in March 1936 and finished correcting page proofs the following August, just over three months after entering the Chapter House at Valle Crucis to begin Glendower.

Morwyn, sub-titled *The Vengeance of God*, is a curious work; incidentally, one of the few modern novels to win the approval of his brother Theodore, who thought it more 'writ from the centre' than his other novels. It describes a descent into hell by the seventeen-year-old Morwyn, her father (a vivisectionist), the narrator of the story and his dog, Black Peter. They are precipitated there by a meteor which strikes the Berwyn Range and carries the block of stone on which they are standing down to the centre of the earth. They find that hell is reserved for the cruel, even those who (like vivisectionists) believe the pain they inflict can be justified. For their sins, they have to sit watching television sets endlessly showing pictures of experiments on animals. This was possibly the worst fate Powys could envisage, as his hatred of TV was such that he would not allow it in the house. It might seem strange that the damned should be able to indulge their wicked vice, but this is no conventional hell: these sadistic shades have the power to harm the living.

Our travellers first encounter the Marquis de Sade and Torquemada, and later make the acquaintance of Calvin and the Roman emperor Claudius Domitius Caesar, otherwise Nero. The Welsh bard Taliesin is there too, but only as a visitor in search of Merlin. The various layers of hell are described in graphic detail, and there are times when torture is described with disconcerting relish.

> Favour us therefore who copy thee and cringe to thee and forever cry upon thy name, favour us who acknowledge thee as our only god; and as for the heretics who refuse to lick the dust before thee — burn 'em, tear 'em, nip 'em with hot pincers, drown 'em, hang 'em, spit 'em at the bunghole, pelt 'em, bruise 'em, dismember 'em, gut 'em, bowel 'em, paunch 'em, thrash 'em, slash 'em, gasp 'em, pare 'em, hew 'em, flea 'em, boil 'em, broil 'em, carbonade 'em, crucify 'em, these wicked heretics!
>
> (*Morwyn*, 319)

Anti-vivisection propaganda it might be, but it is far too close to the private visions of Owen Evans in *A Glastonbury Romance* for comfort.

Sixteen

John Cowper Powys diligently applied himself to the task of learning Welsh in Corwen, taking lessons from a local schoolteacher, Miss Evans. The evidence suggests that his conversational Welsh was limited and barely comprehensible, but with the written word he had more success. He read the Bible in Welsh with the aid of a dictionary and also grappled with the *Mabinogion*: 'the subtlest and loveliest of all mythology after Homer,' in his view. Modern Welsh presented him with more difficulty; he confessed to being unable to read a single word in the journal *Adsain*, asking plaintively in his diary, 'Why is that?'

His standing in the local community was such that he had not only been made a bard of the Powys Eisteddfod but was invited to preside over the chairing ceremony twelve months later. This entailed delivering a speech in Welsh which he composed with the help of Miss Evans. The eisteddfod secretary had bravely invited him to compose and recite an englyn, but after inspecting his efforts a local bard gravely explained all the technical difficulties this verse form entailed: 'all the repetition of inside consonants, their alliteration & rhymes *interior* of the words.' Chastened somewhat, Powys went away to rework his ideas: it would be a Welsh lyric, simpler in form than an englyn.

Phyllis Playter joined in the Welsh lessons, but continued to be prone to depression. Sometimes she felt her life to be merely endurance, and in retrospect she missed what she now saw as the 'margin of recklessness and joy' that attended life in America. Wales had, however, initially come as a relief after England, which she had hated during their sojourn in Dorset. She had gone there expecting a love of England to come down to her from her ancestors 'but instead of this her atavistic feeling made her *hate* it as if her ancestors had shaken the dust off their shoes when they went to America,'

Powys noted. There were days when she suffered a violent reaction against Wales, too, feeling the presence of a demon under the mists, 'a *Vampirizing Dragon* that clutched & clutched & clutched & devoured & sucked the Good up leaving only grasping remorseless Evil!'

The money troubles which afflicted them did not help her adjust. There are constant references to these in the Powys diaries of the late 1930s, and John took pains also to make a new will which ensured that Phyllis would receive some protection in the event of his death; we must remember that his wife Margaret was still living. The presence of Phyllis's mother and aunt next door was not an unmitigated blessing. As Morine Krissdottir points out, she found the management of two houses difficult and had to care for her aunt during illness (PATD, 260). Local characters, however, spring to life in the diaries: not least the town crier, who ('like Culpeper') confided the Welsh names of plants that cured uncomfortable ailments like piles and boils. The countryside around was a constant delight. Powys notes how, on his morning walk one December day, he disturbed a heron, 'a wonderful sight ... which flew away with enormous flapping wings and legs trailing behind — just as at Shirley my Father used to describe to us how to know a heron!' On at least one occasion the landowner, Admiral Cotton, sent a man 'who the T.T. said resembled Mr Quilp' to see how these celebrated tenants of his were getting along, and afterwards 'the TT' (still his favourite way of describing Phyllis) scolded him for 'confiding in gushing intimacy all our secrets to this sinister person'.

The intimacy of John and Phyllis themselves is the subject of many entries in the diaries. Thus, within the first week of their arrival in Corwen:

> 22 May 1935: Up at 7 after holding the T.T. with Indiscribable [sic] Satisfaction of an extremely wicked vicious lecherousness but, at the same time, *heavenly* rapture!
>
> 27 May: Up at 7.40 after holding the T.T. and making love to her in her sleep from which this morning I believe I got more erotic pleasure than I have ever had in my whole life. Think of waiting *till I was 63 and in Wales* — to enjoy the greatest vicious and satyrist pleasure I have ever had! But what heavenly luck that I have a girl — a real ballad-girl whose form can give me these magical thrills!
>
> 28 May: O unknown Reader if you haven't played the Satyr with a girl you have had for ten years you have no idea

of the thrilling pleasure I have got.
(NLW Ms)

The 'unknown reader' of the diaries might feel uncomfortably guilty of voyeurism in being asked to share vicariously in such sensual satisfactions, and one might well wonder what motivated this strange man into looking over his shoulder, as it were, at the wraith of the future reader contemplating this 'satyrish' behaviour. After the sexual failures of his early manhood, did he feel the need to prove that he, too, was capable of experiencing the joys of love? The manner of his love-making with Phyllis is beyond reckoning, but significantly he refers on occasion to making love 'à la Lulu,' which can be interpreted as one sees fit.

Reading John Cowper Powys's diaries and letters is like listening to one half of a conversation; we long to hear Phyllis speak with her own voice. It is clear that she was a woman of great strength and high intelligence, utterly devoted to the man whose life she had decided to share knowing that marriage to him would almost certainly be impossible. In the social context of the 1920s and 1930s, this ranked as bohemianism of the most explicit kind. That she was no mere supporter of his endeavours but an active participant in his creativity is obvious. She not only encouraged him to write certain works, and discouraged the writing of others, but was (at his invitation) a constant critic and advisor, a kind of domestic editor helping to shape his novels in the course of their creation. A woman once with literary ambitions herself, she sublimated these so as to assist unstintingly in his own development as a novelist. There is no knowing what he might have achieved without her; but we must accept his own valuation of her as a woman on whom he depended utterly during the period of his life when his genius attained its full flowering.

No ordinary woman could have done it; and Phyllis Playter was as extraordinary as John Cowper Powys in many respects. She too had a taste for the occult, engaging at times in automatic writing which she believed to be inspired by the spirit of her dead father. John was uneasy about it, fearing that 'an Elemental of a dangerous sort' might be taking possession of her pen. In February 1937, he noted that she had 'a queer feeling of being ... interfered with by some super-natural power — being possessed by something — she explains it by some bad news or some agitating letter.' He added that it was some time since she had experienced anything of this kind: 'It is a physical feeling which she is psychic enough to *get* but not to know its cause.'

The third member of this unusual household was the black cocker spaniel which had accompanied them through all their domestic changes since its birth in New York in 1927. The name by which it was known altered with age: originally Peter or The Black, it had become The Old Black or The Old and was eventually The Very Old. It accompanied its master on his walks, its early exuberance slowly leeching away as time with its attendant ailments took its toll. In February 1939 the dog was afflicted with a growth in its bowels and its steadily downward progress is painfully documented in the Powys diary. It was given morphine by the veterinary surgeon, who also took out some of the bad teeth which were suspected of being the cause of its bronchitis and heart condition. Starkly, on Tuesday 28 March, we read: 'The Old Dies'. Its master had caught a look in its eye the night before so wretched that he had decided to ask the vet to put it out of its misery. Nevertheless, he took the dog for a walk.

> O how slowly paw by paw of his four legs he walked home by my side. He stopped to cough once or twice. I told him of my decision to call the Vet to kill him. I told him that Oscar said we all kill the thing we love. For the last few days he has been abstracted from us absorbed in the mystery of dying — and alone like all of us when we die.
> (NLW Ms)

The Old keeled over in the kitchen and died. 'The T.T. wraps him in her quilt. The T.T. puts the goatskin in his grave ... We went out in snow and chose his burial-place.' The grave can be seen still, thanks to the efforts of Harry and Millicent Lewis, occupiers of 7 Cae Coed in the mid-1990s, who on taking over the property cleared the grave of the undergrowth which had almost totally obscured it. The slate tombstone placed there by John Cowper Powys and Phyllis Playter reads: 'The Very Old. The Black. Born Poughkeepsie New York 1927. Died Corwen North Wales. Greater love hath no man.'

The couple grieved over the pet that had meant so much to them. Phyllis had no heart for gardening next day, though her new plants had arrived.

> So much of her existence side by side with 'the Man' has been

> poured into that Old black form that she feels that her life is cracked and rent in some way. As for 'the Man' he is more selfish and tough and hard and impervious — But at the same time he do think and think of the Old continually. There has rarely been among people of the human race a love equal to that — a devotion equal to that — an obsession equal to that — which the Old had for 'the Man'. I see his face all the time.
> (NLW Ms)

Visions of death haunted them. Visiting The Old's grave, John pictured the dog lying below, wrapped up in the patchwork silk quilt of bright colours; looking at the sunset, Phyllis was moved to declare eloquently that personal life could not simply vanish into annihilation or have anything to do with the corpse. By the year's end, there was not only the toll of another world war to mourn but the death of the brother whom John loved above all others. On a Saturday morning early in December 1939, Llewelyn died at Clavadel in Switzerland.

There had been some warning. Alyse, Lulu's wife, had written to say that he had taken no nourishment for four days because of a stomach ulcer; ironically, after fighting TB practically all his life, it was the ulcer that was killing him. John thought of going to see him but confessed that he was too cowardly to do so. The fact that Gamel Woolsey, Lulu's former mistress, was visiting John and Phyllis at the time may also have helped to dissuade him from making such a long journey, which would have severely taxed him. The end came on 2 December, when a telegram arrived as the three of them were breakfasting together. 'I imagined what it was and said the words, "Lulu's dead,"' John's diary entry reads; Llewelyn had, in fact, died at 6am that day. All three sat heavily, scarcely taking it in.

> Nature made us numb and dumb and cold ... and cold and calm talked of what Alyse would do with the Body. *Whose* body we hardly took in — the word we need on the whole event is not forthcoming — for it is Lulu's own word we need; the word of Lulu, who has died so many times that we cannot believe it now ... I have been wrestling in prayer for him by his photo and at the Rock on the Left where I pray for my son; and now, but only dully and stupidly. I did just now but Lulu wouldn't like that pray [sic] for his soul. I shall *never* do *that* again!
> (NLW Ms)

Llewelyn was, in fact, cremated in Switzerland, but his ashes were brought back to England after the war and buried on the Dorset downs near Chydyok. He was the third of John's siblings to die, the early death of his sister Eleanor in 1893 having been followed by that of his brother Albert Reginald in 1936. Typically John, without a grave at which to mourn Lulu, created his own memorial in Corwen, by carrying a stone up the mountain to add to the cairn he had already created in his honour.

The daily walks continued without The Very Old. After four years in Corwen, John Cowper Powys had a mental map of the area which resembled no other. Particular trees, stones and other features of the landscape had attained especial significance, just as they had at Phudd Bottom in New York State, where he had communed with the souls of long-dead Red Indians. He felt that in Wales he had found his spiritual home. The mass of its people were, in his view, 'more ancient and indigenous than most of our mixed European races.' He saw them as pre-Celtic, descended from Iberians who had established peaceful village communities long before the warlike Celts came on the scene. Their language had in it 'something of that strange elemental rhythm I catch in Homer ... nearer than ours to the primeval voices of hill and forest and river and moorland.'

> They are without doubt *the least advertized race on earth.* Like the Chinese, whom they resemble both in the extreme antiquity of their civilization and their passionate reverence for a scholarly traditional language more rigid and elaborate than the one in ordinary colloquial use, they have acquired the art of wearing an exquisitely polite mask in the presence of 'honourable strangers' eager to pluck out the heart of their mystery.
> (OC, 61)

It was this introversion which, in his opinion, made them so different from the Irish, who were so zealous in proclaiming their 'Irishness' to the world. In contrast, the Welsh habit was 'to *sink inwards,* to hide up from the rest of humanity all that is deepest and most sacred in your soul.'

Surprisingly, perhaps, given the generally extrovert nature of Americans, he found a strong resemblance in some aspects of life between the people of Wales and those of the United States. This lay, however, in what he called the element of 'poetical snobbery' in both peoples: 'an ideal of life free from the snobbishness of class and yet full of imaginative discrimination.'

Some of his reflections on Wales and the Welsh seem a little dated now. In the wake of the Welsh Language Society campaigns from the 1960s on, and with the increase in nationalist sentiment, Welsh people tend to be less passive about their Welshness than they were in his time. There is, too, something in his assiduous analysis of the Welsh character that many might find patronising and irritating.

Yet he writes from the standpoint of admiration, mixing predictable comments on Welsh emotionalism and love of poetry and song with astute awareness of the effects of economic deprivation.

> The economic distress in Wales, the passing away of so many of her native industries, the migration into England of so many of her ambitious sons, has thrown the task of keeping alive the traditional flame of national life into the hands of the masses of the people. This phenomenon cuts, so to say, both ways. It makes Welsh culture at once a very democratic thing, free from the snobbishness of an exclusive middle-class education, and a thing whose higher or more recondite levels fall naturally into the hands of a comparatively small group of extremely learned scholars at the Welsh colleges. Between these two there is a gulf; precisely the gulf that is filled in England by the humanistic, snobbish, and more or less classical education of the upper-middle-class.
> (OC, 81)

For all his sympathy with the Welsh and his understanding of their historic injustices, and for all his sense that he was one of them by reason of ancient pedigree, John Cowper Powys was always seen by the Welsh people among whom he lived as an outsider: an upper-class English gentleman, with a public school accent and impeccable manners, eccentric in ways peculiar to his class, well-meaning and courteous to a degree. But a stranger nonetheless, in the parlance of Thatcherdom 'not one of us'. This says something, not so much about the narrowness of Welsh people as about the ways in which we are identified and placed by our neighbours. It was John Cowper Powys's triumph to win, not only the respect and (to some extent) the affection of the 'ordinary' people of Corwen and Blaenau Ffestiniog, but the acceptance and admiration of Welsh scholars and artists who recognised his achievements and found his allegiance to Wales both a novelty and a cause for satisfaction.

Seventeen

James Hanley thought of John Cowper Powys as 'the man in the corner,' one who stood clear of the mainstream. 'Powys was always conscious of the thin glittering carrot that is held out to the human donkey. Let the world keep on progressing, he is buried in his own. Powys grew inwards. Within himself was his own light-house, his own mine' (AMITC, 3).

It was an inward journey that Powys made when creating the second of his great Welsh historical romances, *Porius*. The setting is the Wales of the so-called Dark Ages that followed the withdrawal of the Roman legions from Britain, but to find it he dug deep into his own psyche. The lack of historical sources provides Powys with the freedom to extend his imagination to the utmost. The result is a novel blending history with myth in a startling amalgam which is as unacceptable to some as it is inspiring to others.

The novel, which in its original form ran to 1,589 pages of type-script, is set in the year AD 499. Remarkably, all the action takes place within the space of a week. The name of its eponymous hero appears to have been inspired by a discovery he made while walking in the depth of winter, for Hanley tells how, 'on a mountain path he came upon a stone slab, upon which was written "Porius stood here"' (AMITC, 6). The actual Latin inscription read: PORIUS/ HIC IN TVMVLO IACIT/HOMO -RIANVS FVIT. The incomplete word has been variously interpreted. In a contribution to *The Powys Journal*, Richard Maxwell recalls Powys's dismay at discovering that the inscribed stone he stumbled on was a mere copy, the original having been stored away when the area was being used as an artillery range (*The Powys Journal*, vol 4, 103).

Porius, as fleshed out in Powys's imagination, is the only child of Prince Einion of Edeyrnion (the ancient name for the part of Wales where Corwen lies) and his wife Euronwy, who is the cousin of King

Arthur. Einion himself has honourable lineage as the great-great-grandson of Cunedda, the Brythonic chieftain who came down with his sons from what is now Scotland to conquer North Wales. The novel begins arrestingly, with the image of Porius standing upon the low square tower above the southern gate of Mynydd-y-Gaer, looking down on 'the wide stretching valley below'. At once we encounter the Powys trick of bringing the homely into the historic, for as he gazes at the tree-tops Porius mechanically murmurs the words, 'Eternus, Edernus, Edeyrn'.

> He was thinking of the way the old Roman, his mother's father, from whom he had received his own name, would always catch them up over the pronunciation of such a word as 'Eternus' and make them repeat it in the correct Roman manner.
>
> (*Porius*, 3)

The nature of the society in which Porius lives is immediately explored. The forest-people, originally Iberians from North Africa, are under constant threat from the Gwyddyl-Ffichti, a ferocious clan whose hold on the district had been ended by Cunedda a century earlier. There is an external threat from the Saxons, who are poised to invade the Vale of Edeyrnion. The Saxons are themselves opposed by King Arthur, described in the novel as 'the Emperor of Britain'. The huge cast of characters includes Merlin, known here as Myrddin Wyllt, who is Arthur's Counsellor, Nineue (Tennyson's Vivien), the enchantress loved by Merlin, the poet Taliessin [sic], 'Head Bard of the Isle of Britain,' and the Modrybedd, three aged princesses who are incongruously known as The Three Aunties, for all the world as if they were a vaudeville act. Aboriginal giants, The Cewri, linger in the mountains of Eryri (Snowdon).

Porius poses difficulties for all but the most devoted admirers of John Cowper Powys. Most of the first chapter, more than 10,000 words in length, consists of densely-packed prose which is relieved by dialogue only in the last few pages. We learn all we need to know about Porius's antecedents and the historical background to the drama which is about to unfold, but effort is required to follow the argument. Those who persevere have their rewards, such as in descriptions of landscape which are quintessential Powys.

> It was one of those peculiar afternoons that arrive in late

> October or early November in this district and are entirely dominated by one natural phenomenon alone — the phenomenon of mist. Wavering and fluctuating in its advances and retreats, and only tangible to the sensitive skin by a faint impact of wetness and chilliness, the mist rises, it would appear, by its own volition, or by the will of the divine water, straight out of the river, and unaffected by wind or sun assumes, weak creature as it is, the dominant and mastering control of a whole unreturning day. This rape of a day by the weakest of her children was more significant of that spot than any other of Nature's methods.
> (*Porius*, 7)

The ghostly colour which the far-off stubble fields imparts to the mist is a theme taken up, set aside, and taken up again with symphonic subtlety, and one of the strengths of the novel rests in physical description of all kinds. The clothes people wear are portrayed with a vivacity and attention to detail more usually found in women writers than male, and the familiarity which Powys seems to possess with the customs and manners of a time so remote from our own can be startling. He makes us absolutely convinced that things were indeed as he describes, though he might be wildly mistaken. Who can tell? Once more he has created, as in *Owen Glendower*, a world parallel with our own, where people talk in exactly the same tone of voice as ourselves. We are at once in the year 499 and in our own time.

The risks Powys takes would appal a less confident author. Merlin looks like a herdsman and speaks in a hoarse, guttural whisper, 'like someone who had given up for long years the use of human speech.' Equally surprising is the portrayal of Arthur. As Glen Cavaliero has pointed out, 'He is presented as a professional soldier first and foremost, and not a hint of the Arthur of later legend is given ... The treatment is not only anti-dramatic, but anti-romantic as well.'

The conflict between Christianity and paganism is one of the themes of *Porius*, and the theological disputes within Christianity is another: Brother John, who lives by the Fountain of St Julian high in the mountains of Eryri, has been a disciple of the heretic Pelagius. We look in vain for what might be called a continuing storyline, but readers with stamina will allow themselves to be led contentedly through a spacious world illuminated by Powys's imagination. Like *Owen Glendower*, the novel is set in an era of change and thus speaks to our own ever-changing times. 'As the old gods were departing then,' wrote the author in his introductory notes, 'so the old gods are departing now.'

Porius took at least seven years to write and was conceived over a much longer period. Writing to Louis Wilkinson, Powys confessed that it suited his 'whimsies and quimsies and de quincies, all my superstitions, prejudices, blasphemies and blissphemies, my hoverings round and my shootings off, my divings down and poppings up'; language uncannily like that which Dylan Thomas employed in his letters. Yet it caused him heartache in that his publishers, The Bodley Head, demanded huge cuts which reduced its length by 500 pages; and even then they were reluctant to bring it out. Salvation came in the person of Malcolm Elwin, who persuaded Macdonalds to publish it in an abridged form in 1951. A much fuller version of *Porius*, taking in hitherto unpublished material, was brought out by Colgate University Press in the USA, under the editorship of Wilbur T. Albrecht, in 1994.

Powys himself believed *Porius* to be his masterpiece, but many would quarrel with this. Its faults are on as grand a scale as its conception, yet the creative force that sustains it and the vigour of its prose are huge accomplishments in a writer who, at the time of its publication, was in his eightieth year. George Steiner believes the novel to combine a 'Shakespearian-epic sweep of historicity with a Jamesian finesse of psychological detail and acuity.' The last word on *Porius* should come, perhaps, from the author himself, who as he revised the ending (an event in itself, since he hated revision), confided to his oldest of friends, Louis Wilkinson:

> The truth is, yes, the truth is that, tho' I am a bit of a moral coward & a bit of a physical one too, I am curiously and profoundly such an instinctive & reverted & atavisticated cave-man that I am far more at home in the year 499 than in the year 1948.
>
> (LTLW, 244)

Any account of Powys's years in Corwen would be incomplete without reference to his friendship with the poet John Redwood Anderson, which was of great importance to both men. Anderson, whose work is now almost entirely forgotten, went to live in Corwen in 1943, but had corresponded with Powys since the late 1930s. A scholarly man, he had been educated privately in Switzerland and later in Brussels, where he studied music. Later he became a headmaster in Hull.

Richard Burleigh has revealed that Anderson was 'a gifted conversationalist with a great capacity to arouse new interests' in people. In this he resembled John Cowper Powys, whom he visited every Saturday. Anderson lived in The Square in Corwen in rented rooms which Powys likened to 'a junior Fellow's rooms at one of the universities'. He excelled in reading his own poetry, which ranged from the philosophic to the elegiac. Powys felt comfortable in his presence, not least because they shared an upper-middle-class background. 'I do not know one of this class for miles around, save old Redwood Anderson, our poet from Hull,' Powys notes in a letter to Louis Wilkinson. Anderson had a certain sang-froid, avoiding agitation even when his sitting-room caught fire from a lighted cigarette he had dropped into his chair. His coolness on this occasion persuaded Powys to call him 'the most masculine person I know,' and to speculate 'with all my essentially feminine mind what I'd feel about him if I were a woman.' Perhaps it is as well that Anderson was not a mind reader.

Anderson appears to have left Corwen around the year 1950, making occasional visits to the town thereafter. By this time Powys was a widower, his wife Margaret having died on 28 February 1947. His diary entry for that day — a Friday — records that his son Littleton Alfred Powys had wired him with the news, obligingly informing his father that 'I need not come to the Funeral on Tuesday'. The next day, which he noted as 'St David's Day, Gwyl Dewi' and 'Old Redwood's Birthday,' he wrote:

> This is the day after my wife's death. In my last letter to her I told her how I remembered the Green Ribbon which she always tied to her mandoline & in her last letter to me she — or the antepenultimate — she praised my essay on Don Quixote. We exchanged very affectionate letters these last few months of her life. But my son tells me I need not come to see her buried.
>
> (NLW Ms)

In a letter to Louis Wilkinson written the following Wednesday, Powys declared that he had 'no idea' whether any of his family save Littleton Alfred had attended the funeral in Bath. He added: 'My son has said that ere long he will come and see me & tell me all, which will be better, he implies, than writing long letters, & I agree.' So, with the minimum of fuss, a marriage which (in spite of everything) had endured for a month short of fifty-one years came to an end. John Cowper Powys did not shock the chapelgoers of Corwen who already believed Phyllis Playter to be 'Mrs Powys' by formally tying the knot, although there was no reluctance on his part to marry her. He did in fact propose marriage, only to be met by a flat refusal. 'She was too proud,' he would say, taking great pride himself in her decision. They were, as the old saying had it, married in all but name. 'Our anniversary for we are now Husband (me) Wife (the T.T.) by Common Law,' reads his diary entry for 25 March 1953.

It was, in fact, their fortieth anniversary, their ruby wedding had they been a married couple. They were contented with one another but increasingly disenchanted with Corwen. Their neighbourhood was becoming more crowded, the development of a post-war council housing estate taking away some of their sense of privacy. The natural friendliness of the newcomers was not entirely to Phyllis's liking: she grumbled that 'it's all very well having neighbours but it comes to something when you can't go to your own dustbin without having to pass the time of day with someone.'

The year was blighted most of all by the death of Theodore Francis Powys, third senior of the Powys siblings. John recorded it in his diary on 27 November in capital letters: DEATH OF THEODORE. He noted that Theodore's last portentous words, 'I shall come back', had been uttered 'very slowly'. John Cowper Powys's physical remoteness from his remaining family in Dorset, and his increasing frailty, again precluded any serious thought of his attending the funeral. He declared himself, in fact, 'very satisfied' with the account of the funeral in the copy of the *Dorset Echo* sent him by Mrs Meech, who lived in Dorchester and typed all his manuscripts for publication. What had upset him far more on the day of the funeral, he confessed in his diary entry of 3 December, was the way their neighbours — 'not our new neighbours — are cutting down the lilacs ... and a holly will probably go too in order to build a wall between our houses.' This indicates not so much lack of feeling for Theodore as the extent to which the petty irritations of life in Cae Coed were fraying the nerves of John Cowper Powys and Phyllis Playter.

Something else was depressing John: his son's illness. After a motor-cycling accident, Littleton Alfred had developed a wasting disease in his muscles. Two days after Theodore's death, John noted how he had kissed a plant 'by Theodore's stream' and 'prayed O so earnestly to my wife Maggie Lyon to take all pain and all discomfort away from my son.' It was around this time that the young Catrin Puw Morgan observed in amazement his passionate outburst against the nuns whom he believed to 'love suffering', described in chapter nine.

As that troubled year of 1953 drew to a close, John Cowper Powys penned a perceptive note inside the back cover of his diary:

> To Theodore the most important discovery in life is and always has been God. His world is a world set as it were at some remove from reality but always with a true correspondence to reality, a symbolic or allegorical correspondence. There is often a strange suggestion of medievalism or Gothick art about his work. His characters are sometimes like gargoyles sometimes like sculptured souls. No writer could be less contemporaneous — his sense of mystery, his awe, his sense of good & evil, of beauty & horror, were utterly foreign to all varieties of literary taste in the earlier years of the present century. It needed the 1st World War to clear the way & the same catastrophe was needed to clear the way for Donne.
> (NLW Ms)

He was paraphrasing the thoughts on Theodore which Louis Marlow expressed in his collection of essays, *Seven Friends*. By this time, however, Powys's diaries had for the most part become a scarcely coherent jumble. They record the small change of life as well as matters of huge import, the taking of hot baths and enemas, the state of the weather. The words are written long-ways, cross-ways, along margins, in any available space, and are occasionally broken up with odd drawings of faces or other things that take the writer's fancy. It seems, one moment, that the octogenarian is at last succumbing to second childhood, but the next he surprises us with an acute observation. It reminds us that, old as he was, he remained a professional writer practising his craft. The words continue to flow as ceaselessly as the river Dee. Yet, with the completion of *Porius*, his great work was now done. He would write several more novels, none of which would attain anything like the stature of those by which he made his reputation. These fantasies include *The Inmates*, which tells of the incarceration of a sexual fetichist in a mental home called Glint; his Homeric novel *Atlantis*; *The Brazen Head*, set in a fanciful thirteenth century Wessex; and *Up and Out*, which he himself described as 'a sort of Mythical Skit on the Space-adventure Tales of today's fashion'. Even as a 'skit' it scarcely rates as science-fiction, being a rambling fable about the survivors of a nuclear war. His last novel, *All or Nothing*, was published in 1960, the year in which he achieved his eighty-eighth birthday. Some further short fantasies were posthumously published.

The 1940s and 1950s saw, too, the appearance of further non-fiction of the philosophical or quasi-philosophical kind. *Mortal Strife* appeared in 1942, when the outcome of World War Two was still in doubt, and reflects the mood of the times, often descending to mere propaganda. *The Art of Growing Old*, published two years later, is a more considered work, concluding with the stoical thought that such are the limitations of our minds that at the last our attitude must be one 'of cheerful ignorance and of fearless expectation'. *In Spite Of* (1953), a self-styled Philosophy for Everyman, develops familiar arguments in an attractive and good-humoured way. The basic premise is that in spite of specialist thinkers of many kinds, who set themselves up as guardians of particular truths, we are entitled to devise simple ways of coping with life's complexities and difficulties. If we don't wish to do it for ourselves, old John Cowper Powys will do it for us. Have absolute faith in nothing save our awareness of self, he tells us, the 'I am I' that provides the sense of our own separate identity. The key word is 'enjoy,' which Powys uses in a special way. When he tells us to enjoy life, he does not wish us to engage in a shallow pursuit of pleasure but to cultivate a sense of forbearance and detachment. This, he believes, will enable us to find satisfaction even in the most unpromising circumstances: we can 'enjoy' even people we despise, by observing them humorously and trying to understand what motivates them. It is a philosophy far easier to enunciate than to practice, and one wonders whether the man who penned such lofty thoughts really succeeded in 'enjoying' the neighbours in Cae Coed who caused him such vexation as the 1950s advanced.

Powys certainly needed all the philosophy he could muster as he was assaulted by one blow after another. His son, Littleton Alfred, died on 16 February 1954 and was buried in Bath three days later. He did not attend the funeral but, that morning, set out at 8.15 on a walk that lasted five minutes short of two hours. On a gloomy, misty day with occasional sleet he stood facing the stone he had long ago dedicated to his son. His thoughts he kept to himself but 'all was Black Darkness on every horizon.' That evening, writing up his diary, he wondered: 'Did any of us go to my son's funeral?' It seems an especially poignant thought.

The following year, on 27 September 1955, his brother Littleton Charles died, the sixth of his ten siblings to go to the grave before him. His diary entry next day combines tenderness with brutal honesty.

> Littleton died yesterday at 8.10 am just as I was setting out for Cwm Bowydd & this was the day I lay under a stone between the Ghost-tree and the drive. And I thought of Old Littleton being with me there ... Today I did not think of Littleton at all ... which shows what a heartless sod I am.
> (NLW Ms)

Eighteen

Since John Cowper Powys's entire life was a journey into the unexpected, it is perhaps apt that he should choose to spend his last years in the dour slate-quarrying town of Blaenau Ffestiniog. It is impossible to say quite when he decided to live there, or exactly why he made this unusual choice. Blaenau has its virtues, but it does not generally attract the middle-aged or elderly who have no pressing need to settle there. Set high amid the mountains and moorland of the Snowdonia National Park, it is one of the wettest places in the British Isles, the nearest meteorological station of Crib Goch registering an average annual rainfall of more than 4,200mm. Its sturdy grey stone houses have dignity and character, but the face which the town presents to the world is one of resilience rather than warmth and charm. By the 1950s the decline of the once-flourishing Welsh slate industry had already deposited huge piles of waste around the edges of the town. The community was even more closely-knit then than it is today, with the Welsh language predominant in all social activities. This meant that people with little or no spoken Welsh at their command, such as John Cowper Powys and Phyllis Playter, were unable to share fully in the social and cultural life of the town. Without a car, or even the ability to drive, they might well have felt isolated in an alien land. Yet John Cowper Powys seemed quite at ease there, and even after his death Phyllis Playter chose to remain in Blaenau rather than seeking a more obviously congenial town or city.

Perhaps the answer is that Powys did not see Blaenau at all, but a town of his own imagining, as much ancient Greek as Welsh. It was, he informed correspondents such as Louis Wilkinson and Benson Roberts, 'a perfectly Aristophanic town'.

> For it is indeed *exactly* without exaggeration like the Nephelo-cuccugygia the Cloud-Cuckoo-Town described in '*The Birds*'

of that Athenian Comedian! What a good word by the way for birds the word *orthithes* is!
(LTBR,101)

The decision to leave Corwen after twenty years was dictated partly by annoyance with their new neighbours and by a sense that they were too accessible to casual callers, who could reach this small town easily by both road and rail. But there were more romantic reasons, seated in Powys's acute feeling for history and mythology and his sense of his own personal destiny. For Blaenau was much closer to Snowdon itself, the majestic Yr Wyddfa — to give it the dignity of its correct Welsh name — where Porius had gone at the climax of the novel of that title.

> And as he swung his arm backwards and forwards he felt that this highest peak of Eryri must indeed have been named yr Wyddfa, 'the Tomb,' by destiny itself. He decided that it must be one of the four great gates into that World of the Dead to which Brochvael had once told him certain Cis-Alpine Gallic tribes used to offer large four-square barley-cakes made without milk and without the shedding of blood. He felt as if he stood on an earth-crust that covered a cosmogonic cavern wherein the bones and ashes and the mouldering dust of gods and men and beasts and birds and fishes and reptiles had been gathered into a multitudinous congregated compost, out of which by the creative energy of Time new life could be eternally spawned; spawned, it might be for the use of other universes, when this one had been dissolved.
> (*Porius*, 870)

Gerard Casey, who with his wife Mary played a major role in the search for a new home, has noted the importance of Mount Snowdon in Powys's imagination. In a conversation with the author of this book, he recalled that during walks on the Berwyns near Corwen, Powys would become 'very excited' at the distant prospect of Snowdon.

> Legend had it that Merlin had finally disappeared on Snowdon. He [Powys] said that if possible he would like to move nearer Snowdon .... He said, 'Get as near to Snowdon as you can and get me a house to live in.' The nearest place we could find was in Blaenau Ffestiniog.

The troubles with neighbours in Corwen appear to have reached a climax on 5 September 1954, when Powys noted that 'the T.T.' had been 'awfully upset' by car wheels going over 'the Round Bed where she had planted things' and turning it into mud. The following day's entry in his diary reads:

> This is a Momentous day in the life of the T.T. & her old man for we are now boldly & frankly confessing to everybody that we intend to leave here ... as soon as we have found another Welsh home! And we are now begging every body to help us in this! For we don't want a house. We only want a sitting room and bedroom combined no kitchen no bathroom but a good toilet or WC.
> (NLW Ms)

He was 'all for Blaenau', he confessed, a trip there by car with his friends John and Elena Puw Morgan having at least influenced his choice if not persuading him finally. Their daughter Catrin recalled that in her mother's view it had been a disastrous outing, with rain sheeting down and mist obscuring much of the view, but Powys had reacted quite differently.

> Afterwards I heard him say, 'I'll never forget going there the first time. It was like going to Mount Olympus because of the swirling mist. You saw these houses and you knew they must have been full of very special spirits.' He said it was the most striking place he had ever seen.

Phyllis Playter sometimes accompanied Gerard and Mary Casey on their house-hunting excursions to Blaenau Ffestiniog, declaring herself 'very pleased with the Blaenau Post Office & with the Blaenau Boots the Chemist', according to John Cowper. He himself drove to Blaenau one day 'with Mrs Morrison the shop' and was thrilled with it. 'Yes I will be obstinate to live there ... it was Cloud Cuckoo Heaven,' he wrote in his diary.

The house eventually selected had a downstairs sitting-room and scullery and an upstairs bedroom. It was 1 Waterloo, one of a pair of two-storey stone-built quarrymen's cottages in the Manod area of Blaenau Ffestiniog. 'Blaenau is fixed,' his diary entry for 25 September reads. 'We have decided to take that half-cottage of Stone and Buy it for £165 & then do it up to suit us for another £165 if not more!!' The move was made on Wednesday 29 September 1954, John Cowper declaring Phyllis to be 'absolutely heroic'. The journey turned out to be venturesome, for having reached Bala by rail from Corwen they discovered that there were no trains to Blaenau for two to three hours. The stationmaster obligingly phoned for a taxi so they arrived in Manod in style, taking a late breakfast at The Don café after paying the taxi driver a 'very very reasonable' fee. 'I had a raw egg and eat [sic] some dry stale bread I brought in my pocket. The T.T. had bread & butter & we shared a Pot of tea.'

Thus their last great adventure began, one that lasted until John Cowper Powys's death nearly eight years later. Blaenau appears to have provided a happy conclusion to his life, although anyone objectively viewing his choice of 1 Waterloo might have had serious misgivings. Far from providing the distance from neighbours which his troubles at Cae Coed appeared to require, he was surrounded by them. There were people living next door, and this pair of cottages stood amid a higgledy-piggledy maze of similar dwellings just off the main road. To the rear, however, was a track leading up the bare hillside, down which a mountain stream cascaded past the cottage occupied by Powys's next-door neighbours. Fortune favoured him, too, in that the people of Manod were neither unduly inquisitive nor resentful of strangers: in fact, there was a fairly constant influx of them, as workmen taking jobs in the quarries arrived with their families.

Powys and Playter were especially fortunate in their next-door neighbours, the Roberts family. David Roberts was a self-educated quarryman with a strong interest in politics, his communist sympathies striking a chord with Powys. 'Our salvation is coming from the East,' Roberts would say, meaning the Soviet Union. He was also a chapel-goer, combining Christian beliefs with communism without any sense of complication. His son Llewelyn, then an adolescent, performed odd jobs for Powys such as painting shelves and hanging pictures: these included a small painting of the Rev Charles Francis Powys. Llewelyn Roberts, who later became a local government officer, recalls how John Cowper Powys and Phyllis Playter would sometimes call in to see them on a Sunday afternoon.

> Mr Powys would sprawl in a chair opposite my father's. He always wore a colourful waistcoat and a corduroy jacket. My father would exchange cigarettes with Miss Playter, who often brought records in to play on our gramophone: classical music, a lot of it with an American background. I would say that Mr Powys put up with the music rather than enjoying it

> thoroughly — though I can remember him liking a record we played him of *canu penillion*.
>
> When my father was very ill, John Cowper Powys went upstairs to see him. I don't know what he said but it sounded as if he was preaching. He made my father feel a lot better. I know he wasn't a Christian, but in one sense he was more of a Christian than many I've met. I feel privileged to have known him.

Powys and Playter appear to have been right in thinking that there would be fewer casual visitors in Blaenau than in Corwen. The people who made tracks for 1 Waterloo generally did so by invitation. They included Jacquetta Hawkes, author and archaeologist and wife of J.B. Priestley (himself an admirer of Powys), the critic G. Wilson Knight and the novelist Angus Wilson. Augustus John went there to paint a portrait of Powys and Jonah Jones to make a sculpture of him. For Powys, John was a god-like figure.

> Augustus John simply thrilled me because he looked so exactly like a statue I've seen of Zeus! When he rose to depart I leapt at him exactly as a devoted Dog of considerable size leaps up at a person he likes, and kissed his Jovian forehead which is certainly the most noble forehead I have ever seen. I kissed it again & again as if it had been marble, holding the godlike old gent so violently in my arms that he couldn't move till the monumental and marmoreal granite of that forehead cooled my feverish devotion. His final drawing was simply of my very soul — I can only say it just *awed* me.
> (LTLW, 337)

Jonah Jones took his three-year-old daughter to Waterloo, and was struck by the empathy between the child and the octogenarian author. Long afterwards, Jones would recall how Powys 'descended to actual childishness' in her presence, talking on her level in order to engage her sympathy. Others who knew Powys at this period retained clear memories of his innate understanding of children. Some close friendships developed with local people, among them the poet Raymond Garlick, then a young teacher in Blaenau Ffestiniog. For Garlick, Powys was 'a Socratic figure', steeped in wisdom. Beside the couch where Powys did his writing, propped up on cushions with his pad balanced on his knee, various objects were laid out on a small table: 'a china owl, the bird of Pallas Athene, an ancient Greek coin, and the elements of his unvarying diet ... a pint of milk, a loaf of stale white bread, a raw egg in a wine-glass, some olive oil and, I think, some sugar' (*Planet* no 110, 52).

The couch was placed by the window in the upstairs room which was, for John Cowper Powys in these final years, sitting-room, study and bedroom. He slept on the couch separately from Phyllis Playter, who lived and slept in the downstairs room. This does not indicate any alienation between them, but simply a physical arrangement which suited them both. In a conversation with the present writer, Garlick noted that 'Phyllis would often sit upstairs with him, sewing, and she would always come up when there were visitors'. Powys's frankness of speech could be disconcerting. 'How beautiful you must look without your clothes on,' he suddenly told an attractive middle-aged woman, a compliment which she accepted gracefully.

In his old age, says Garlick, John Cowper Powys looked every inch an aristocrat.

> He was a very grand-looking man but also very gentle and warm and completely unpretentious. But Blaenau was in many ways a town totally attuned to eccentricity. You could be as eccentric as you liked and Blaenau would have taken you to its heart ... I think that people were rather proud that he had chosen to live in Blaenau. They knew he was a major writer and that also was something that people honoured in a person. It was a highly literate community.

Trefor Edwards, an artist and teacher who also knew Powys during this period, recalls him putting a small object to his forehead while exclaiming 'Oh! Oh!' He was, maintains Edwards, practising psychometry, the divination of facts and events and people from inanimate objects associated with them.

> Now John was telling me that, by placing a small piece of mosaic from the area of Troy to his forehead, he was able to go back to the ten years when the Greek King Agamemnon and his soldiers had fought against the Trojans. He was very serious about it all. I was too inexperienced to be able to participate. John Cowper Powys, however, was inspired to produce his book *Homer and the Aether* (Macdonald 1959). The Aether was able to look down on all that was happening below.
>
> (*New Welsh Review*, no 28, 77)

It was during his Blaenau period that Powys received his honorary degree from the University of Wales and the Plaque of the Hamburg Free Academy of Arts, the German novelist Rolf Italiaander travelling all the way from Hamburg to present the latter to him at 1 Waterloo.

Some saw Phyllis Playter simply as an acolyte, completely dominated by Powys, but others found her memorable in appearance and personality. Thin — indeed 'painfully' thin — racked by a smoker's cough, dressed always in black, she possessed for Raymond Garlick 'a gentleness and grace of movement that gave an inkling of the beautiful woman she had been'. She was as fiercely protective of Powys as ever, capable of dismissing casual callers with insulting abruptness. The Welsh writer Rhydwen Williams would recall how he and Huw T. Edwards, a man of some eminence in public life in Wales in the 1950s, decided to call on John Cowper Powys when by chance they were together near Blaenau Ffestiniog. Knocking the door of 1 Waterloo, they found themselves confronted by Miss Playter.

> 'We would like to see Mr Powys,' they said.
> 'Well, he wouldn't like to see you,' she replied, and closed the door.

By this time, John Cowper Powys had little sight in his right eye and was relying more and more on his companion, who ran hot baths for him and posted his letters on days when he did not feel like leaving the house. Until overcome by infirmity, however, he continued to take daily walks. These often took him past Tan-y-Manod Hall, the centuries-old house inhabited by John Vaughan-Jones and his sister. Powys liked to think of Vaughan-Jones as the local squire, but local people tended to regard him simply as a solicitor's clerk in Blaenau. The unmarried brother and sister were among the closest friends of John Cowper Powys and Phyllis Playter.

The physical world inhabited by John Cowper Powys became increasingly narrow, and his diary for 1961 painfully records the shrinking of his concerns.

> 1 January. The T.T. Shaved me beautifully.
> Then the T.T. washed my face.
> Then she washed my back.
> Then she changed my vest.
> She had already changed my drawers.
> I have already cut my finger-nails.

He retreated into a private world in which he appears to have imagined himself one with the old gods he believed had never died. The diary frequently quotes a passage from Longfellow's poem about the war-god Thor, words he used to chant to himself on his walks.

> 5 January. Mountains covered with white snow.
> Wind due north.
> I stay downstairs.
> I am the God Thor.
> I am the War God.
> This is my Hammer.
> Miolnir the Mighty.
> Giants and Sorcerers cannot withstand it.

On 1 February he rejoiced:

> Hoo-Doo!
> My father was born between today & tomorrow.
> O how lucky we six boys and five girls were in our parents!

Three weeks later, he prayed to Pallas Athena and to Hera 'to guard the T.T.', noting in parentheses that these were 'Zeus daughter and wife those two girl-friends'. On 6 May, he noted: 'We, Miss Phyllis Playter & I, John C. Powys, spent the day alone for no visitors came.' There was a similar entry on 15 May: 'There is nothing to remember that happened today nor anyone who came.' The final entry in the 1961 diary, the last he kept, is dated 7 December and merely repeats the earlier incantation.

> I am the God Thor.
> I am the War God ...

A further eighteen months were to pass before the death of John Cowper Powys at the cottage hospital in Blaenau Ffestiniog on 17 June 1963. This followed an attack of influenza and a period of increasing infirmity during which he abandoned his upstairs room to spend all day lying on his couch downstairs. His lapse into second childhood was such that on his death-bed in the local hospital he contentedly sang the traditional English ballad 'John Peel'. It is impossible to imagine that his death did not come, at last, as a mercy.

His body was cremated in Colwyn Bay and the ashes scattered on Chesil Beach, Weymouth.

Postscript

To some extent, John Cowper Powys is the invisible man of English Literature. Writers of critical works on the twentieth century novel feel it safe to ignore him, because he stands outside the canon. There are endless debates on why this is so. Some would say he is excluded simply on merit, or lack of it. It is true that there are glaring faults in his work. It is often verbose, his circumlocutions sometimes touching depths of absurdity. His prose is frequently clumsy, his ear for dialogue so faulty that he allows characters to make long speeches without interruption. He can be embarrassingly whimsical, and his early novels especially have touches of melodrama which make one cringe.

Yet there are elements in his work which are unique and sublime. He creates characters who live as powerfully in one's imagination as those of Dickens or Dostoievsky. There is, too, a hugeness in his novels, measured not only in length but in conception. They take in a vast range of people and of argument. Philosophical and religious debate sits cheek-by-jowl with matter-of-fact descriptions of basic bodily functions. The depth of his sympathy is astonishing. He suffers the frayed nerves of young women maddened by the obtuseness of their lovers; feels the lust for power and sexual fulfilment of arrogant industrialists; endures the shame and humiliation of those beyond the pale of society; enjoys the innocent pleasures of the very young and the very old. He is the most protean of writers, insinuating himself into the souls of trees and fish and into the dim consciousness of stone walls; compelling us to believe that such consciousness exists, and that it is not only human beings who have souls.

Powys is a caster of spells, and not everyone is willing to be caught up in wizardry. As the twentieth century gives way to the twenty-first, the magical view of life is not fashionable. Yet it is only by surrendering a sense of realism that one can enter his worlds. It is not that he writes fantasy, like Tolkien, but that the real world expands, the universe becomes the multiverse, and people discover powers which, in the realm of scientific testing and proof, they do not possess.

All this is consistent with the sense that Powys experienced, from his earliest days, of being a magician. Yet the very use of the word brings down the shutters which bar so many people from appreciation of his work. This is inescapable, for it is not only an effort of the imagination that is needed to enjoy the work of John Cowper Powys; it is a surrendering of any absolute sense of what is possible and what is not.

It is going too far to say that one either hates the work of Powys or loves it, yet it is true that he tends to inspire an intensity of emotion. His admirers have included George Steiner, G. Wilson Knight, Henry Miller, Angus Wilson and Iris Murdoch, and in his introduction to Powys's *Autobiography* J.B. Priestley described him as 'a major writer, an original, a genius ... quite shockingly undervalued, often completely neglected'. The neglect is partly due to his deliberate choice of a solitary life and his avoidance of London and all metropolitan literary contacts. In the view of a leading Powys scholar, Glen Cavaliero, this resulted in his being regarded as an eccentric and a cult figure; although, in his early American years, his stature was such that he was called upon as an influential witness in defence of James Joyce's *Ulysses*. It was when he began to write in earnest that he became deliberately reclusive. His omission from many literary histories, although deplorable, was a perhaps inevitable consequence of his distancing himself from the metropolis: there are none so insular or parochial as the literary coteries of London. Abroad, he has received wide acclaim in Germany, France and Sweden, and is highly regarded by a number of academics in the USA. His academic reputation generally, in fact, now stands higher than it did. The Powys Society, founded in 1967, has encouraged the critical study of the works of John Cowper Powys and those of Theodore (T.F. Powys) and Llewelyn, through its annual conference and *The Powys Journal*. *The Powys Review*, an independent journal, fulfils a similar role.

In spite of the range of his work, it is as a novelist that John Cowper Powys must be assessed. All else: his critical essays, his philosophising, his poetry, his letters, his diaries: is subordinate to his fiction, which defies easy categorisation. He wrote novels set in earlier times, but they are not in the true sense historical novels. In spite of the wealth of vivid detail they embody of customs, dress and action, they are essentially timeless worlds of Powys's imagining, in which our own ways of thought and expression are given fifth century or fifteenth century settings. It is not that human beings in long-ago epochs did not feel much the same emotions as ourselves, but that in imposing our own diction on them he is wrenching them out of their time. The world they inhabit is very different from our own, but it is a world like no other, a Powysian world which is a gift he presents to all who enter it.

John Cowper Powys was bold in his treatment of sexual matters, as bold indeed as his contemporary D.H. Lawrence, although given far less credit. He brings humour to bear on the subject, in contrast with Lawrence's quasi-religious solemnity. Into the narrative of his novels he wove, too, a wealth of philosophical and metaphysical speculation; wove it even into descriptions of landscape and sky. Occasionally it sits uncomfortably there, but for the most part he rode his luck with confidence, enriching his readers' lives with visions of startling newness and clarity.

Unhappily, the multiverse that constitutes the work of John Cowper Powys had attained rarity value at the time this book was written. The original uncut versions of *Maiden Castle* and *Porius* were available, at a price, and so was a paperback edition of *Wolf Solent*. All the other novels were out of print. It is to be hoped that the major novels, at least, might reappear, to enable fresh generations of readers to enjoy them; and, perhaps, to encourage critics to assess his work anew and to place it where it belongs, not only amid the twentieth-century canon of Lawrence, Joyce, Woolf et al, but into the body of literature that includes Dickens, Conrad, Hardy and Fielding.

Abbreviations

Abbreviations used in the text are as follows:

TPB:	*The Powys Brothers* by Kenneth Hopkins (Village Press, 1974).
WA:	*Welsh Ambassadors* by Louis Marlow (Bertram Rota, 1971).
ABR:	*Apples Be Ripe* by Llewelyn Powys (Longmans, Green 1930).
AGR:	*A Glastonbury Romance* by John Cowper Powys (Macdonald, 1955).
WS:	*Weymouth Sands* by John Cowper Powys (Picador, 1980).
WAS:	*Wood and Stone* by John Cowper Powys (Village Press, 1974).
PTGH:	*The Letters of John Cowper Powys* to Glyn Hughes, edited by Frank Warren (Cecil Woolf, 1994).
WoS:	*Wolf Solent* by John Cowper Powys (Macdonald, 1961).
MC:	*Maiden Castle* by John Cowper Powys (Picador, 1979).
PSN:	*The Powys Society Newsletter* (various numbers, as itemised in text).
AROA:	*John Cowper Powys: A Record of Achievement* by Derek Langridge (The Library Association, 1966).
THOES:	*The Hollowed-Out Elder Stalk* by Roland Mathias (Enitharmon Press, 1979).
TB:	*The Buffoon* by Louis U. Wilkinson (Village Press, 1975).
TBP:	*The Brothers Powys* by Richard Perceval Graves (Routledge & Kegan Paul, 1983).
LTHBL:	*Letters To His Brother Llewelyn* edited and selected by

Malcolm Elwin (Village Press, 1975).

JAF: *The Letters of John Cowper Powys* to Frances Gregg edited by Oliver Marlow Wilkinson assisted by Christopher Wilkinson (Cecil Woolf, 1994).

TGP: *The Great Powys*. HTV drama-documentary written by Herbert Williams and produced/directed by Peter Edwards of Lluniau Lliw Cyf, 1994.

SF: *Seven Friends* by Louis Wilkinson (Mandrake Press, 1992).

COTB: *Confessions of Two Brothers* by John Cowper Powys and Llewelyn Powys (Sinclair Brown, 1982).

VAR: *Visions and Revisions* by John Cowper Powys (Village Press, 1974).

NLW: The National Library of Wales, Aberystwyth.

EA: *Elusive America* by John Cowper Powys edited by Paul Roberts (Cecil Woolf, 1994).

AMF: *After My Fashion* by John Cowper Powys (Pan, 1980).

IDOS: *In Defence of Sensuality* by John Cowper Powys (Village Press, 1974).

PATD: *Petrushka and the Dancer: The Diaries of John Cowper Powys 1929-1939* selected and edited by Morine Krissdottir (Carcanet Press, 1995).

JCPN: *John Cowper Powys: Novelist* by Glen Cavaliero (Clarendon Press, 1973).

ROTPB: 'John Cowper Powys' by Gilbert Turner. From *Recollections of the Powys Brothers* edited by Belinda Humfrey (Peter Owen, 1980).

LTBR: *Letters from John Cowper Powys* to C. Benson Roberts (Village Press, 1975).

OC: *Obstinate Cymric* by John Cowper Powys (Village Press, 1975).

EAJCP: 'The Sacrificial Prince: A Study of *Owen Glendower*' by Roland Mathias. From *Essays on John Cowper Powys* edited by Belinda Humfrey (University of Wales Press, 1972).

OG: *Owen Glendower* by John Cowper Powys (Picador, 1978).

ABBREVIATIONS

AMITC: *A Man in the Corner* by James Hanley (K.A. Ward, 1969).

LTLW: *Letters of John Cowper Powys* to Louis Wilkinson (Village Press, 1974).

Select Bibliography

The major novels of John Cowper Powys, in order of publication, are as follows:

Wood and Stone, 1915; *Rodmoor*, 1916; *Ducdame*, 1925; *Wolf Solent*, 1929; *A Glastonbury Romance*, 1932; *Weymouth Sands*, 1934; *Maiden Castle*, 1936; *Morwyn*, 1937; *Owen Glendower*, 1940; *Porius*, 1951 (first publication of complete text 1994); *The Inmates*, 1952; *Atlantis*, 1954; *The Brazen Head*, 1956; *Up and Out*, 1957; *Homer and the Aether*, 1959; *All or Nothing*, 1960.

His numerous other works include:

Poetry:
Odes and Other Poems, 1896; *Poems*, 1899; *Wolf's Bane*, 1916; *Mandragora*, 1917; *Samphire*, 1922; *Lucifer*, 1956.

Literary studies:
Visions and Revisions, 1915; *One Hundred Best Books*, 1916; *Suspended Judgments*, 1916; *The Pleasures of Literature*, 1938; *Dostoievsky*, 1946; *Rabelais*, 1948; *Powys on Keats*, 1993.

Philosophical books and essays:
The War and Culture, 1914; *The Complex Vision*, 1920; *The Art of Happiness*, 1923; *The Meaning of Culture*, 1929; *In Defence of Sensuality*, 1930; *A Philosophy of Solitude*, 1933; *The Art of Happiness*, 1935; *Mortal Strife*, 1942; *The Art of Growing Old*, 1944; *Obstinate Cymric*, 1947; *In Spite of: A Philosophy for Everyman*, 1953; *Elusive America*, 1994.

Several collections of letters written by John Cowper Powys have been published. The Village Press in London performed a notable service by bringing out many of these in the 1970s as well as reprints of novels and other works.

The Powys Checklist & Readers' Guide by Alan Howe (The Powys Society, 1996) contains full details of all works by John Cowper Powys and other members of the family.

Acknowledgements

Firstly, my warm thanks to Francis Powys, John Powys, the Estate of the late John Cowper Powys and Laurence Pollinger Ltd for their generosity in allowing me to use copyright material.

I am indebted to a great many other people who, either deliberately or unconsciously, helped me write this book. The late Geoffrey Watkins, whose friendship I valued deeply, first aroused my interest in John Cowper Powys by showing me a letter which Powys had written to him in the mid-1950s. Much later another friend, the novelist Richard Jones, gave me welcome encouragement.

I am grateful also to Belinda Humfrey, who early in the 1980s keenly supported an idea I then proposed for a radio programme about Powys. Unhappily this came to nothing, but her willingness to provide information from time to time has always been appreciated. As editor of *Essays on John Cowper Powys* (1972), *Recollections of the Powys Brothers* (1980) and the critical periodical *The Powys Review* she has contributed greatly to Powys studies.

My thanks also to Dr Glen Cavaliero, who as critic, scholar and friend has assisted this project. The author of many works on John Cowper Powys, he was kind enough to read this book in manuscript to check for factual errors and omissions. I am grateful for his pertinent observations, generous praise and constant encouragement, and permission to quote extracts from his copyright work, notably *John Cowper Powys: Novelist*. The views expressed in this book are entirely mine.

Another Powys scholar, Dr Morine Krissdottir, has kindly allowed me to quote from *Petrushka and the Dancer*, her selections from the diaries of John Cowper Powys and provided the photographs reproduced here. She also provided invaluable help in the making of *The Great Powys*, the television drama-documentary which I scripted. Directed by Peter Edwards and produced by Lluniau Lliw, it was screened by HTV Wales in December 1994.

My warm thanks also to Oliver Marlow Wilkinson, whose recollections of his parents, Louis (Marlow) Wilkinson and Frances Gregg, and of his godfather, John Cowper Powys, have been of inestimable value. For an understanding of the relationship between Gregg and Powys, the selections from their love letters which he edited, *Powys: Jack and Frances*, is required reading. Christopher Wilkinson has also been most supportive.

The Powys Society, both through its publications and the help of individual members, has been of great assistance. Apart from publishing *The Powys Journal* and newsletters, it brings out booklets and reprints works by members of the Powys family. My thanks especially to Paul Roberts, whose keen research has shed light on many corners of John Cowper Powys's life. As author and editor, he has produced work of the highest standard. Other members of the Society to whom I am particularly indebted are Isobel Powys Marks, Stephen Powys Marks, John and Eve Batten, Gerard Casey, Sven Erik Tackmark and Anthony Head.

Alun Richards and Joan Stevens kindly provided me with relevant literature. For personal recollections of John Cowper Powys, or critical observations on his work, I must thank (in addition to those named above) Catrin Puw Davies, Llewellyn Roberts, Eigra Lewis Roberts, Raymond Garlick, Gwyn Jones, Trefor Edwards, Roland Mathias, Rhydwen Williams, Jonah Jones and Jeremy Hooker. Many people in Blaenau Ffestiniog and Corwen also provided willing help, notably Mrs Millicent Lewis of Cae Coed, Corwen.

The staff of the National Library of Wales were, as always, the soul of efficiency and kindness, and I am especially grateful to Geraint Phillips, assistant archivist, who has patiently catalogued Powys manuscripts. My thanks also to Andrew Greenwood, senior information officer at the Peak National Park.

John Powell Ward has been a perspicacious editor at my publishers, Seren, and I am grateful to him. Last but certainly not least, my thanks to my wife Dorothy for once again giving me unstinting support and encouragement.

Index

Series Afterword

The Border country is that region between England and Wales which is upland and lowland, both and neither. Centuries ago kings and barons fought over these Marches without their national allegiance ever being settled. It is beautiful, gentle, intriguing, and often surprising. It displays majestic landscapes, which show a lot, and hide some more. People now walk it, poke into its cathedrals and bookshops, and fly over or hang-glide from its mountains, yet its mystery remains.

The subjects covered in the present series seem united by a particular kind of vision. Writers as diverse as Mary Webb, Dennis Potter and Thomas Traherne, painters and composers such as David Jones and Edward Elgar, and writers on the Welsh side such as Henry Vaughan and Arthur Machen, bear the one imprint of border woods, rivers, villages and hills. This vision is set in a special light, a cloudy, golden twilight so characteristic of the region. As you approach the border you feel it. Suddenly you are in that finally elusive terrain, looking up from a bare height down on to a plain, or from the lower land up to a gap in the hills, and you want to explore it, maybe not to return.

There are more earthly aspects. From England the border meant romantic escape or colonial appropriation; from Wales it was roads to London, education or employment. Boundaries are necessarily political. Much is shared, yet different languages are spoken, in more than one sense. The series authors reflect the diversity of their subjects. They are specialists or academics; critics or biographers; poets or musicians themselves; or ordinary people with however an established reputation of writing imaginatively and directly about what moves them. They are of various ages, both sexes, Welsh and English, border people themselves or from further afield.

Spot-on-the-border novels like Bruce Chatwin's *On The Black Hill* or Arthur Machen's *The Hill of Dreams* are not the only border kind. Some writers, like the fiercely other-wordly John Cowper Powys, lived in two places, one each side, and their work was set accordingly. This new study of Powys by Herbert Williams is in two parts, which exactly match these two aspects. Williams lucidly and with colour and comment brings out Powys's later adoption of the Wales he believed he inherited. Powys was a remarkable twentieth century border phenomenon, whose significance this book aims to chronicle.

About the Author

Herbert Williams is a writer of poetry, fiction, biography, TV and radio scripts. He was an award winner in the Rhys Davies Short Story Competition 1995 and was awarded a Hawthornden Poetry Fellowship in 1992.

The Border Lines Series

Series Editor: John Powell Ward

Elizabeth Barrett Browning	Barbara Dennis
Bruce Chatwin	Nicholas Murray
The Dymock Poets	Sean Street
Edward Elgar: Sacred Music	John Allison
Eric Gill & David Jones at Capel-y-Ffin	Jonathan Miles
A.E. Housman	Keith Jebb
Francis Kilvert	David Lockwood
Arthur Machen	Mark Valentine
Wilfred Owen	Merryn Williams
Edith Pargeter: Ellis Peters	Margaret Lewis
Dennis Potter	Peter Stead
John Cowper Powys	Herbert Williams
Philip Wilson Steer	Ysanne Holt
Henry Vaughan	Stevie Davies
Mary Webb	Gladys Mary Coles
Samuel Sebastian Wesley	Donald Hunt
Raymond Williams	Tony Pinkney
Francis Brett Young	Michael Hall